"How does a **20-foot centerboard sloop** take on Superior, the largest Great Lake, the **deepest, coldest,** and **deadliest**? Like a fly in a roomful of swatters. Fulfilling his dream cruise, gingerly tiptoeing from Bayfield to Thunder Bay, Marlin Bree is often whumped back inside the infrequent breakwaters by almost daily thunderstorms It's a lake whose square waves can flex thousand-footers three ways—especially in a Northeaster. Up from the pages emerges an aura of distance, dispersion, absences; a **cleanliness** and **poetry;** and above all, a cold, windy presence determining all. **Fascinating**."—**Sail** magazine

"...a **tense, exciting and harrowing** account of a lone sailor against the sea. This **great sea story**, though, is more than just a fine adventure. Bree uses his voyage as a vehicle to *explore man's relationship with the lake,* recount its history and delve into its legends. He packs the book—as he packed his boat, to the gunnels—with the **legends** that have created such a special aura around the lake, from **famous shipwrecks,** lost **gold mines** and **great storms** to the almost unbelievable story of the world's richest silver mine. The book is **not to be missed** by anybody who loves adventure or delights in the Great Lakes."—*Flint (MI)* **Journal**

"...a nice comfortable read, clearly, unpretentiously written and loaded with lore and interesting anecdotes."—**Star Tribune**, *Minneapolis, Minn,.*

"Lake Superior is the largest body of fresh water in the world. Some call it the most **dangerous**. Bree learned that even on the calmest of days the weather on Superior must be watched with diligence, and the weather that scares even the most experienced boatmen is a storm from the northeast. Bree's small craft was caught in one of these Northeasters as he traveled north along the Minnesota coast. The author's description of this storm **will set your teeth on edge**."—**Rocky Mountain News**, *Denver, CO.*

"Although the type of voyage that Bree undertook is a far cry from sailing the Chesapeake Bay or even the Atlantic, salt water sailors will relate to his trials and find his account of them **a good read**....Bree has found new grist to grind for a crowded literary genre—**sea stories.**"—Barrett Richardson

"...a story of travel and adventure with strong narrative pull. It also makes a substantial literary contribution by digging under the surface to explore our economic losses and the still uncertain future of this region. ...Bree keeps looping back to the myth of the *Fitzgerald* to underscore the irony that enriches the twin themes of adventure and understanding. A **strong read**".—**MSP Airport News**

"...a comfortable, entertaining, two-evening read that should have **special meaning** to anyone who has lived on or near the big water...If you have ever held your own on a rolling deck in a Lake Superior storm, or wished you could, *In the Teeth of the Northeaster* is a living recollection of one man's communication with that greater power everyone must someday face."—**Evening Telegram**, *Superior, WI.*

"**...an uplifting portrait** of the people living in this little-known frontier and a uniquely American story imbued with the spirit of the great outdoors."—**Eastern/ Southeast Boating**

"...a **great read** and shared experience!"—The **Bulletin**, *Shoreview, MN.*

"Bree said that perhaps his **greatest challenge** in writing *In the Teeth of the Northeaster* was to get across that **indescribable** Lake Superior feeling. That's the **mystique** that grabs even those who have never sailed its waters."— **Daily Press**, *Ashland, WI.*

Also by MARLIN BREE

BOAT BOOK

BOAT LOG & RECORD

ALONE AGAINST THE ATLANTIC
by Gerry Spiess with Marlin Bree

IN THE TEETH OF THE NORTHEASTER

A SOLO VOYAGE ON LAKE SUPERIOR

BY MARLIN BREE

MARLOR PRESS, INC.

MARLOR PRESS, INC.
4304 Brigadoon Drive, Saint Paul, Minnesota 55126

CONTENTS

FOR THOSE

WHO LOOK OVER

BIG WATERS

—AND DREAM

AND ESPECIALLY

FOR

LORIS & BILL

I
STORM OVER SUPERIOR

I RUBBED MY EYES WITH COLD FINGERS AND WATCHED the lighthouse at the breakwater fade into the distance. My masthead light winked out its red, green, and white warning as I probed deeper into the lake. In the predawn darkness and fog patches, I could feel the waves more than see them. Something in my mind kept repeating danger, danger, but I tried to ignore it. Sailing Lake Superior was as much a mental battle as a physical one.

"Hello ... Security ..." I called on my VHF radio. "This is the sailboat *Persistence* leaving Two Harbors on a northerly course of oh-four-oh. Over." I repeated my message several times, then flipped the switch to receive. There was only a white hiss.

I picked up my damp chart to double check my course and wrote down my compass heading and estimated speed. It was 5:19 A.M. I had just passed the Two Harbors lighthouse. Finally, I was on my way up the north shore, from Minnesota to the Canadian border.

I had been on Superior for a little over a month—since embarking on the Fourth of July from Bayfield, Wisconsin. I intended to sail as much of the world's largest freshwater sea as I could over this summer, to circumnavigate its 2,900 miles of inland shoreline, if possible.

I had been warned that I could sail Superior's north shore from mid-July to mid-August, but after that, the lake couldn't be trusted. Now I had to hurry; I was behind schedule.

Superior's damp chill penetrated my heavy nylon parka, wool sweater, and long underwear. I huddled down in the open cockpit. Though it was midsummer, the big sea has a way of draining a person of bodily warmth. I told myself that this was what solo sailing up north was all about— getting up in predawn hours for a stretch of calm water before the lake began kicking up. High waves or worse inevitably came with fierce winds in late afternoon. Lake Superior was infamous for its quick-rising storms that sank even the most modern steel freighters. I reminded myself to be off the lake by 3:00 P.M., when the storms usually rolled in.

Persistence began to be lightly bucked by rolling swells of dark water. I glanced at my watch: 6:58 A.M. Then I switched on the Kenwood transceiver and tapped out in Morse code, KAONTC . . . KAONTC de KAOTCU.

I swayed from side to side in my boat, listening. Somewhere out there, safe on shore, Loris, my wife, was hunched in front of her radio, trying to tune in my signal. The picture filled itself out in my mind: nearby, and nearly underfoot, our oversized Shetland sheep dog, Angus, would be lying. In his bedroom, our thirteen-year-old son, Bill, would probably be half awake, listening for the dits and dashes that signified all was well.

Minutes had passed between transmissions. I grew anxious. Something in the atmosphere was blocking the radio signals. If I couldn't get through, Loris would start to worry. Frustrated, I snapped off my radio and turned my attention back to navigating. The silver of fog and sea turned into utter blackness.

As if by magic, a glowing red ball appeared on the horizon. Dawn was approaching. The sun bored its way through the fog and cast blood-colored rays upon Superior's dark waves. I hoped that it would burn off the fog, but then I remembered the old sailor's warning, "Red sky at morning, sailor take warning."

The bow suddenly sliced into a wave crest and a torrent of white water was racing along the deck. *Persistence* shuddered at the impact and momentarily halted. I ducked, then swung the tiller to starboard to let my boat fall off a few degrees and find a better angle. I plunged ahead, but the seas were growing difficult.

Slowly the day brightened and the big sea turned a brilliant blue flecked with whitecaps. In the distance, I could see the shore, edged by foaming surf. Beyond the reefs, the green shoreline climbed quickly into the Sawtooth Mountain range. Wisps of vapor hung over the pine forests. A dark, almost black, patch of land or fog—I couldn't tell which it was—lay on the horizon.

As I sailed onward, I began to sense something ominous in the air. I turned my face to the breeze, trying to find what direction it was coming from. It seemed to lie just beyond the dark mass in front of me.

The wind was swinging around now, a bad sign. I had been warned repeatedly about the northeaster—a storm that roared down from Canada, building up fierce winds and waves over hundreds of miles of open water. I swallowed hard. If the wind shifted just a few more degrees, it would be from the northeast. And that meant not just any storm, but the one I dreaded.

By 8:46 A.M., the dark mass on the horizon seemed to be growing larger. My binoculars were not helping much, but I figured it was just a strange fog bank. I turned back to the business of making passage, bracing the tiller with my knee to hold my course as I consulted the chart. I saw that Castle Danger was off my port beam and ahead lay Gooseberry Reef. Split Rock lighthouse, with its reefs and shipwrecks, would not be far up the shore. I also noted the waves were still growing ominously.

"Damn," I swore. My calculations had confirmed the worst. "We're averaging only two knots."

At this sluggish speed, my hopes of reaching Canada today were dwindling, and in fact, getting close to nil. I'd have to face it; I might be forced to turn around and try again tomorrow.

I needed to eat. Securing the tiller to let *Persistence* hold the best course she could, I went below to the cabin to rummage about for a cookie. It would be my long-overdue breakfast.

When I climbed back to the cockpit, the fog bank had taken on a strange rolling motion, no longer just extending off the shore and onto the lake. It was now moving toward me in many dark shapes, like huge black bowling balls. Gusts of wind slapped my face.

I glanced up at *Persistence*'s telltales. They flapped harshly. There was no longer any question.

I was in the direct path of a northeaster.

Persistence reeled from side to side, taking water over her beams with each roll. The waves were speeding up and giving nasty shoves. This was dangerous; if she were caught broadside, she might capsize.

I had hoped we could get back to a port of refuge before the storm grew to full strength. But it was clear now that the waves and the wind were overpowering my little boat. I was trapped—the only thing to do was to take down the sails and ride out the storm.

I left the protection of the cockpit and clambered to the cabin top. Wind screamed in my ears, rattling my parka and tearing at my glasses. I grabbed for the boom, braced myself with one hand, and uncleated the mainsail. But in the grip of the gale, the sail was taut on the mast and it would not slide down. The boat broached atop a roaring wave. I lurched and fell. There was a stabbing pain in my side I had to ignore. I got up, tore at the whipping, flapping sail, and stuffed it into the waiting shock cord.

Next the forward sail. I stumbled toward the jib controls. I had to be quick and move between waves, or the big sail might twist around itself and become a lethal kite that could drag us down into the violent waters.

Carefully timing my action, I readied the two jib furling control lines, clenching one with my teeth. Then I pulled them as far as possible; moments later, the jib was secure. I breathed a sigh of relief but knew I was a long way from being safe.

The wind and sea were still slamming *Persistence* about. If I didn't get momentum and gain maneuverability, one of the wave trains could catch us and fling us over. The waves had grown huge. Somehow, *Persistence* lifted her stern before each wall of water could crash into the cockpit and overwhelm her.

I could feel the water's coldness on my face as I leaned out over the transom to swing down my 5-horsepower Mariner outboard. A wave splashed me, obscuring my vision. I grabbed the starting cord and yanked.

The small engine howled into life; *Persistence* plunged ahead. We ran wildly, almost surfing through the growing waves. With luck we'd make it back to Two Harbors.

S . . . s . . . s . . . something hissed. I turned around to face a huge wall of water running across the other wave trains. Rogue wave! In minutes, its foaming white crest towered above me and crashed with a roar into the transom, shoving *Persistence* sideways.

I jammed the tiller over, feeling the rudder bite and groan. My bow slid around at a crazy angle in the face of the wave. *Persistence* careened over, then lay on her beam in the onrushing fury, her mast sticking into the wave.

We were helpless against the wave's power.

Another wall of green loomed above me.

"No!" I screamed. I tried to steer away, but it smashed us broadside, spinning and tipping us. I twisted my body about and raced the small outboard to full power. *Persistence* strained to climb the next wave. At the crest, her stern pitched into the air, her propeller spinning helplessly. Then we began to slide down, down the green slope, picking up momentum.

Trying to keep my bearings, I turned my spray-covered glasses to shore and could barely discern a white structure. I had seen it before, somewhere close to the harbor and lighthouse I was seeking. The Two Harbors entryway couldn't be far off.

A white haze began wisping about, and then, before my startled eyes, the building disappeared and my entire world turned white. I could see nothing beyond the plunging bow. I felt the cold wind on my back, heard the howl of the gale-force winds. In horror, I realized I had gone from storm to fog bank.

Ooom-paah! Ooom-paah! Disoriented by the fury of the northeaster, it took me several moments to realize that I was hearing the entryway foghorn. Obediently, I began steering for it and then I froze. The sound was coming from the wrong direction—from the sea, not from where land ought to be.

I checked my compass—I was still on the right heading. I broke into a cold sweat. Fear swept through me. Had I become totally confused in the fog? Was my compass heading in error? Would I end up on the reefs?

"So long as I have water under my keel, my boat is safe," I repeated over and over. Terrified, I made the only decision possible. With a great force of will, I shoved my tiller over to head away from land—forcing us deeper into the raging lake.

I was alone in the white haze, rushing nowhere, then suddenly, everything grew bright about me. I roared out of the fog bank and into a sunny day. In the distance, I could see a long stone seawall and, at its tip, the lighthouse and entryway—my safe harbor.

Immediately I steered for it, fighting my way over the waves, until what seemed like hours later I was inside the harbor, tying *Persistence* to a steel barge.

I blinked in the glare of sunlight and sudden heat, aware that my clothing clung to my body, drenched with sweat and lake water. My hands were shaking and I could hardly stand upright. I felt dazed. The boat's American flag fluttered softly in the light harbor breezes, while just outside the breakwaters the storm raged.

My arrival had not gone unnoticed. A man walked over from the dock and peered down.

"Where did you come from?"

"Out there," I said, with an unsteady wave of my hand. "I'm sailing around the lake."

"You've been out *there*?" he glared at me. "Anybody who goes out on Superior is more than a little bit crazy and downright stupid, too!"

"You don't understand," I finally managed to answer. "Tomorrow I'll try again." Slamming the hatch behind me, I went below.

He stood for a moment, staring down at my small boat, then looked out at the raging storm.

I knew what he was thinking—yet there was so much more to my voyage, in fact to my dream, than I could have ever explained.

2

THE
DREAM
BEGINS

IT WAS MORNING, POSSIBLY IN EARLY FALL. LAKE SUPE-
rior's air and water had a delicate, almost crystalline quality and stillness. As if in a dream, the lake, shoreline, and
sky were in muted, pastel colors, each blending into the
other. Gliding out of the mists was a large but fragile-look-
ing canoe made of birch bark. The paddlers were Voyageurs, legendary canoemen of the north country. They
seemed to be silent and reflective, lost in their own thoughts,
their faces lifting upward, as if they had heard something
on the distant shore.

I had taken that mystical voyage often, if only in my
dreams. I was not on Superior, but at the Minnesota State
Historical Society, standing in front of an oil painting over
the building's sweeping stone stairway. The picture was so
real that I could almost sniff the fragrance of the deep
north woods and the freshness of Superior's waters.

I was on my way to the director's office; if all went well,
in several months I intended to be navigating through that
frontier of rocks, sea, and sky. I would be a modern-day
Voyageur, following some of the original lake routes of Superior's earliest explorers. It would be a fascinating and
even faintly romantic voyage for a history buff and nature
lover like me.

"**I** 'll start my voyage at Bayfield, Wisconsin," I began after clearing my throat, "and sail the Apostle Islands. Then I'll make my way down the western shore of Wisconsin, spend some time in Superior's largest ports—Duluth and Superior—and then voyage up Minnesota's north shore to Thunder Bay, Ontario. From there, if wind and weather permit, I'll explore more of the lake."

Russell Fridley, the Minnesota State Historical Society's director, made a steeple with his fingers as I spoke.

"I've been interested in the lake for years. I think of it as one of America's last frontiers. Now I want to get to know it the only way I really can. And that is slowly, from the deck of my own sailboat."

"Have you sailed Superior before?" Fridley asked.

"Sure," I said. "I've skippered keelboats a couple of times around the Apostle Islands. I've been sailing for about ten years. But on this voyage, I don't plan any daredevil sailing. If Superior gets rough, I'll just get off."

Fridley seemed to relax. "And what specifically do you need from us?"

"Background material. Whatever will help me understand more of Superior's history. I'd especially like books I can carry along. Not much has been published lately that I can find."

"I'm a fan of the lake myself," Fridley said. "And there's a treasure trove of history on the lake that hasn't been touched. Did you know that there is an island on Superior that once was the richest silver mine in the world?"

He paused a moment. "When are you planning to begin your voyage? We'll get some material together for you to take along."

"The Fourth of July," I said. It came out with more assurance than I felt. "I plan to begin my voyage on the Fourth of July."

As I steered my elderly car down the long hill past the Historical Society building, the immensity of my project began to overwhelm me. I wanted to sail at least the western shores of the world's largest freshwater lake in one summer, which I figured I could do if I sailed hard and the weather was good to me. But that was just the physical part.

More important was the knowledge I hoped to uncover. A lot of Superior's past had been lost over the centuries, just like in the painting of the Voyageurs paddling off into the mists. Sailing would let me get close to the world I wanted to see, and, in fact, slow everything down and make it more manageable.

This was a special summer for me—I had worked hard to set it aside. And sailing was the only way to accomplish what I wanted to do.

The setting sun burnished the wood an amber hue. Back at home now, I admired the boat I had prepared for Superior as she lay on her cradle beside my house. Above the veneered teak deck rose the graceful mahogany cabin with its dark-colored portlights and hatch covers. I put my hand out to touch the wood; it felt warm and smooth. My hand lightly caressed it as I walked along one side.

She was not large—just 20 feet overall—but she looked strong and beautiful. Piece by piece, I had built this boat with the finest woods I could find. I was her creator. I knew her intimately, from her mahogany ribs to her laminated western red cedar hull, from her white oak keelson to her Canadian birch plywood cabin sole.

While I was building her, my neighbor, Gary Ewings, used to walk over on nights like this to review my progress. "You're really working on a piece of sculpture, not just a boat," he'd say. I'd laugh a little, but he was right. Building the boat was special to me.

I worked not only during the pleasant evenings of spring and the fresh summer days, with the sun beating down on my back, but also in the winds of fall and the cold of winter. In the northern climes, where summers are short, the test of a dedicated boatbuilder comes between November and April.

Some days I had to shovel my way through 6-foot snow-banks before I could climb on board in my heavy parka, snow boots, and mitts. But once inside the boat, I sometimes couldn't work. All I could do was sit—the battle to get there had exhausted me.

In colder temperatures, nothing seemed to run right, including electric drills and saws—they shrieked and howled like banshees. My boat was entirely glued with epoxy, which required heat to set. The worst problem was getting the glue to dry. I finally solved the problem by using my wife's hair dryer to blow hot air on the glue. This worked great, but if I left too soon in the subzero Minnesota cold, the epoxy would still be in its semigummy form when I came back—and would probably remain that way until spring.

Regardless of the season, globs of glue often covered my clothing and sometimes even got into my hair. I had to cut patches and chunks out with scissors. Even the doorknob to the front door of our house became sticky with the stuff. But that was useful. When the doorknob didn't stick to my hand, I knew that the glue on the boat also was dry.

Because I built outside, I had to stay alert for rain clouds. If they appeared, I'd rush to finish up and cover the wood. But many times, the rain splattered down on me, ruining what I had just finished. After a big rain, I'd spend hours throwing water from the bottom of the boat. One neighbor had a running joke about making the boat into a swimming pool.

But summers were best, for that was when people would gather around to chat as I worked. Mark, our *St. Paul Dispatch-Pioneer Press* newspaper carrier, would walk up the driveway, sometimes with his younger brother in tow, to admire my boat as only a fourteen-year-old could.

"It's beautiful," he'd say, coming over to peer inside the hull as I worked. And he'd add, meaning to be complimentary, "It looks like a real boat, too!"

"Where are you going to sail?" a neighbor would ask, on a detour from a walk with his dog.

"Oh, I don't know," I'd say, conservatively. "Probably, one of the local lakes like White Bear or Minnetonka. She's just a little centerboard boat that only draws about four and a half inches of water."

"You're not going to sail the ocean, are you?" they'd eventually ask, referring to our Minnesota adventurer, Gerry Spiess, who had built a plywood boat in his garage and then sailed the Atlantic. I had written a book with him—they were worried some of his dreams had rubbed off on me.

"Definitely not," I answered emphatically. "This isn't *Yankee Girl* (Spiess's boat) or even a Great Lakes keelboat. Any stormy wind or heavy waves might tip her over. She's just a little boat," I usually added with a laugh. Then they'd look admiringly at my boat and get kind of quiet. Something in their eyes would tell me that they were thinking about being out on a beautiful lake.

"How long did it take?"

I wasn't proud. I'd clear my throat and say, "Seven years."

Part of the reason it had taken me so long to build the boat was because I had not been content merely to follow standard design specifications. I imagined my little boat shoving her way through the millions of waves she'd encounter in her lifetime. I'd see her in a storm, carried aloft by a huge wave, slammed down so hard her timbers shook. Then I'd think of a way to build her hull even stronger, just in case. But that was easy in a wood veneer boat—all you had to do to get more strength was add more layers of wood.

Though small, my boat would be tough. I built her out of western red cedar veneers, which I'd special-ordered from a mill in Oregon. The veneer "plank" was only ⅛ inch thick—and nearly as light as the balsa wood in model airplanes. The day my case of veneers arrived, I held one up and it nearly went sailing off in a breeze. But from these wafer-thin veneers would arise a sturdy, durable high-technology hull, in which every piece was epoxy-glued to all other woods in a strong monocoque design.

Each row of wood went on at a 45-degree angle to the keel—in all, three layers. I'd clamp the wood veneers to the hull's form with staples until the superstrong epoxy glue dried. There were tens of thousands of staples in that hull. Then came the truly god-awful and tedious part of building a veneer hull. After the glue set, I had to pull each staple out by hand.

I'd used white oak for the keel, and when it came time to cut a slot for the centerboard, I found out how tough that wood was. First, I tried my electric drill; the drill bit burned up. Next, I tried a hand brace and a bit, but the edge soon dulled and would not cut. My electric saber saw broke blades on the tough oak as if they were matchsticks. In desperation, I tried the electric drill again, but with a small bit—⅛ inch—then enlarged the opening with a keyhole saw. Finally, I began cutting with the only tool I had left—a handsaw.

After about ten minutes of aerobic-type exercise, I had cut about an inch and a half—discouraging progress—but I was determined. I began to pace myself. In the morning, I'd go out first thing for a round of furious sawing. I'd go out again in the late afternoon and again in the evening. It took a full three weeks for my saw to chew through all the wood. On the last strokes, I waited for my moment of triumph. But as the saw finished its cut, the heavy centerboard slot remained locked in place. It did not drop to the floor.

I stared unbelievingly at the saw marks. Exasperated, I hit my fist against the wood, but it remained wedged. I looked closer: my saw cuts had wavered. The strain on my saw blade had bent it to one side, interlocking the wood in place.

In a fury, I slammed an ax into the slot. Wham! The entire hull beneath my feet flexed with the blow, vibrating for moments afterward. But I noticed this time the stubborn slot moved a fraction of an inch.

I wrestled a 5-foot-long steel bar into the opening, and finally, with a groan, the slot fell to the floor. I slumped, panting heavily. A horrible thought struck me—in my frustration, had I splintered the wood or cracked the glue joints, microscopically fracturing the hull? I crawled underneath, inspecting my boat with my hands and eyes. Finally, I breathed a sigh of relief. No breaks, splinters, or cracks.

"If nothing else," Loris said wryly when I came in the house, "you've got a tough hull there."

Soon it was time to name the little boat.

"*Wave Thruster*," said my son, Bill.

"*Petrified Eagle*," I said.

But Loris and Bill shook their heads.

I frowned. Perhaps I was being *too* democratic about the whole damned thing. After all, it was *my* boat. Maybe the family didn't need to be this involved.

"You've been working on that boat for a long, long time . . . with great persistence," my wife told me. "It deserves a special name." She suggested we write our favorite ones on a piece of paper. We tacked this list to the kitchen cork wall and looked at it for the next several weeks.

In the end, a name emerged that symbolized the boat . . . the project . . . and a whole lot of other things.

My boat became the *Persistence*.

As the boat grew in complexity and strength, Loris had become concerned.

"The storms," she said. "You know Superior is notorious for its quick storms."

"I'll carry a VHF radio tuned to the weather stations. I'll watch the horizon and if something comes up, I'll get off."

"The waves . . ."

"If it's bad, I just won't go out."

She shook her head, then gave me a patient, wifely look. "If you get caught out there . . ."

"I have a tough boat, you know. I'll be careful. I promise."

"Well, I'll still worry. You'll have to get a ham radio license. And agree to contact me first thing in the morning, and after every day's run."

I began to study Morse code.

Though I had built *Persistence* carefully, there was no telling how she would handle. To find out her capabilities, I began sailing alone on local lakes. A lot of other people became interested; soon I started to get some advice.

A weekend warrior advised me from the window of his Mercedes, "Be sure to get sail off in a hurry if weather comes up—don't ever get caught with everything up." Another veteran sailor inspected my outboard engine, then shook his head. "You should have an inboard," he advised. "Outboards on Superior get cracked heads, split plugs, and soaked ignitions—and end up not working when you need them most."

One day an old friend came out to visit my boat. *Persistence* promptly squatted under our combined weight. "Sits a little low in the water," he observed. "Otherwise, she's a beautiful boat."

Even more chilling were the rather blunt words of a sailor I met: "The Coast Guard doesn't encourage yachtsmen to carry EPIRB's (Emergency Position Indicating Radio Beacon)."

I looked at him in surprise. I knew they were considered standard safety equipment for blue-water sailors. "You've only got about twenty minutes in those waters," he said, shaking his head, "so nobody'd get to you in time."

I listened to them all, but continued my own testing. I was beginning to learn things about my boat.

Because I did not have a speedometer, I used a tubelike device that had to be inserted in the water. While one hand remained on the tiller as I sailed, I would lean over the side of my boat and stick the knotmeter in the water to learn how fast I was going.

Persistence turned out to be relatively speedy for her size. On her fastest point of sail, she could do almost 6 knots. Tacking into the wind, she could get nearly 5½. Of course, I was sailing a bare boat—one without any stores in it—and I knew she would slow down when she got loaded up. I also knew Superior's waters would not be the relatively calm seas of these inland lakes.

As I experimented, I was delighted to learn that I had a secret weapon for Superior—if I pulled my centerboard up and ran my 5-horsepower Mariner outboard at about half throttle, I could do over 6 knots. This was surprisingly speedy for a little sailboat, and it made me feel more confident about spending time on the big lake. Speed meant safety. If I got into any trouble, all I had to do was turn up the engine and roar into the nearest port.

I had intentionally chosen sails that I could reef substantially and quickly. My 104-square-foot mainsail had not one, but two reef points. In high winds I could cut its size to only 50 square feet—little bigger than a beach towel. My forward sail, a genoa mounted on a Cruising Design furling device, had control lines leading back to my cockpit. In seconds, I could vary the amount of sail from "all up" to only a few square feet of storm sail.

As the weeks of testing came to an end, I looked for winds as strong as I could find, short of a tornado. The boat would lean over only so far, then she'd stiffen up. We'd go right on sailing.

Late in June, I winched *Persistence* onto her trailer and parked her in our driveway. I spent several more weeks working far into the night, installing my radio gear—a VHF (Very High Frequency, for short ranges) and an HF (High Frequency, or ham, long-range transceiver)—as well as antennas. But that meant I'd use up a lot of electrical energy.

My problems were solved by the suggestion of a friend at GNB, a battery manufacturer. Why not try the sun? I mounted two solar panels on the cabin top and two Stowaway batteries in the bilge. I hoped the solar panels would give me enough charge to cruise throughout the summer. But just in case, I also packed an AC battery charger.

Loris helped me stow provisions. We filled the bilges with cases of canned food like Dinty Moore beef stew, chili, and Spam. Dr. Charles Mayo, my physician at Group Health, donated a medical kit, with the diplomatic advice: "You may not need this for yourself, but perhaps you can be of aid in an emergency where you're going."

In the tiny galley, I mounted a single-burner butane camping stove, and beneath my bunk, a small marine portable toilet. But there was still more to get in, for I wanted to be totally self-sufficient on board my little boat, dependent on no one for my needs, especially since there would be nobody to depend on.

At midnight on July 1, almost exhausted, I stowed twenty-eight charts of Superior, batteries, tools of all sorts, spare rigging wire and fittings, Norwegian pile undergarments, polypropylene underwear, sweaters, knit wool caps and bags of clothing, blankets, and a sleeping bag. I added in life preservers and a Stearns "survival" suit—in case anything went wrong. On top of everything, I piled in reading material for the voyage, including a history book published in 1944, *Lake Superior,* located for me by the Minnesota Historical Society; the official *United States Coast Pilot: Great Lakes,* various cruising guides, plus a *Reader's Digest* book of great sea tales, and my old portable typewriter. If I had the time, I planned to do some writing.

As I climbed down a stepladder to the ground, I saw in the glare of the garage lights that my trailer's wheels were bulging. Begun as a lightweight pleasure craft, *Persistence* was now a vastly overweight cruising vessel.

But we were ready, my boat and I. We would begin our voyage on the Fourth of July.

Superior—the greatest lake of them all—awaited.

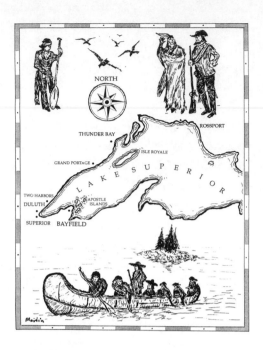

3

RETURN TO THE LAKE

BY LATE AFTERNOON OUR CAR WITH *PERSISTENCE* IN TOW crested the hill of highway 13 in Wisconsin. It was a golden, bright day and, as the trees along the shore thinned, I could look out upon the huge blue waters of the big lake. Below, the road began to squirm and twist along the rocky shore-line, finally dropping in a steep descent to the historic old fishing village of Bayfield.

Conversation was slow and listless. "Don't forget to tell me where you are," Loris said. "Stick to your radio sched-ule—I want to hear from you every day at seven A.M. and ten P.M. on the forty-meter band."

"I'll remember," I said for the umpteenth time. I didn't want her or Bill to be concerned.

"I'll worry about you."

"Don't. *Persistence* and I will be okay."

She went back to her own thoughts as I turned on the car radio. But soon I was hearing the mournful chords of Gor-don Lightfoot's song, "The Wreck of the *Edmund Fitzgerald*":

The legend lives on from the Chippewa on down
Of the big lake they call Gitche Gumee—

Superior they said never gives up her dead
When the gales of November come early.

I half listened for a while as the lyrics described the 729-foot vessel's mysterious disappearance. The *Fitzgerald* had sunk with the loss of all hands in a Superior gale only ten years before. I did not need to be reminded that even modern steel ships, built especially to withstand storms and crewed by professional sailors, sometimes did not survive this lake.

I switched stations, only to tune in a newscast about a man lost overboard on Superior. "He was sailing alone and is now presumed missing," the radio newsman said. "Authorities found his sailboat, and on it, his dog. But his body has not been recovered."

A chill ran down my spine. He was missing somewhere in the waters of my first destination, the Apostle Islands. I tried to look unconcerned as I stole a glance at Loris. If she'd heard, she did not show it. Perhaps, like me, she just didn't want to discuss the tragedy.

I stared out the car window at the lake stretching into the horizon, so huge I could see the curvature of the earth upon it. Today, it was a picture-postcard lake. In the distance, beneath cottony white clouds, three downbound oreboats glided like brightly colored toys. Superior's far edge blended into the blue sky. This was sweet Superior, the queen of the freshwater lakes, who drew millions to her shores each summer.

But Superior had other faces as well. Old sailors' tales tell of a "crack" in the lake into which countless boats have fallen. This is the north woods version of the "Devil's Triangle"—a way of accounting for the disturbingly large number of maritime tragedies. One estimate is that nearly five thousand vessels rest in Superior's dark waters.

In that greatest of all American seafaring yarns, *Moby Dick*, Herman Melville wrote: ". . . these grand fresh-water seas of ours . . . are swept by Borean and dismasting waves as direful as any that lash the salted wave. They know what shipwrecks are; for, out of sight of land, however inland, they have drowned many a midnight ship with all its shrieking crew."

There are many explanations for Superior's darker side, but the further one probes, the more mysterious seems the disappearance of so many boats, ranging in size from sturdy sailing vessels to steel ore carriers—even World War II pursuit boats. In its violence, this northern lake can flip a huge tanker's stern so far out of the water that its giant propeller only lashes helplessly in the air. And under certain conditions, it can bend, twist, or even tear off a modern ship's steel parts.

The statistics are also alarming for the Great Lakes in general. During a two-decade period on these freshwater seas, from 1879 to 1899, about six thousand boats were wrecked, of which about one thousand went down with a loss of all hands. As William Ratigan points out in *Great Lakes Shipwrecks and Survivals*, "Nowhere in the Atlantic or the Pacific is there an expanse of 90,000 square miles to muster such a record of death and destruction."

Superior is known worldwide for its quick storms, which can build up mountainous, steep seas of fresh water. This is a different sort of wave, and wave pattern, from that a sailor would encounter in the ocean: square-shaped wave trains with frontal walls of fresh water that roar down on a ship. These peculiar storm conditions could catch a ship broadside to capsize it or stress it so much that the hull itself can crack.

In the 1600s French explorers had voyaged in fragile birchbark canoes through a wilderness route up the St. Lawrence and the Ottawa rivers into Georgian Bay, and then over the top of Lake Huron. They were seeking the Northwest Passage to China, carrying presents in their canoes for the Emperor of Cathay. One explorer stepped ashore near Green Bay, Wisconsin, wearing a robe of China

damask embroidered with birds of paradise over his buck-
sins and moccasins in case he should meet a Chinese prince.
Though in either hand he carried pistols.

The early explorers did not discover the riches of the Orient; their journey took them instead to a body of water so
huge they thought they had found an ocean.

"Though its waters are fresh and crystal, Superior is a
sea," one Frenchman wrote. They called their discovery "le
Lac superior," meaning the big lake above Lake Huron. But
as time went on, the French name was Anglicized, and the
more apt definition of Superior emerged.

Upon its vastness, early explorers reported seeing two
moons riding across the heavens. Some nights, the dark
skies came alive, dancing with mysterious spirits—the
northern lights. The explorers described islands big enough
to grace any kingdom, sometimes floating in the sky; at
other times arising from the sea upside down, seeming to
balance on their dark, wooded peaks. As if by magic, the
enchanted islands appeared and reappeared in the distance,
luring men on.

Soon fortunes were being wrested from the New World by
those bold and adventurous enough; for two hundred years
the lake area would be the source of a rich fur trade. One
explorer returned to Quebec in "New France" from his
two-year voyage at the head of a 360-canoe caravan laden
with furs. But there were also tales of lonely outposts, of
men driven wild by the north country, of hunger and freezing, and of the incredible bravery of the Voyageurs paddling their long canoes as they plied the watery highway of
the north, carrying trade goods to the last outpost of civilization, Grand Portage, on Superior's north shore.

Onto Superior's shores came yet another brand of fortune
hunter—the "black robes." These French priests—Jesuits,
Recollects, and Sulpicians—were following their evange-
listic calling, intending to consecrate a wilderness five times
the size of France. They traveled in canoes, sometimes hiking alone along woodland paths, to erect birchbark chapels

and to set up the altars they had carried strapped to their backs.

At times, they were in pain; often they went hungry. One woodland priest, after eating only rock moss and one of his moccasins during six days, nevertheless felt rewarded for his privations—he had been able to baptize an Indian child who died of hunger, saving it from "the burning." Sometimes, the black robes were savagely tested in their faith by Indians who tortured them, among other ways, by chewing off their fingers joint by joint.

The Jesuits' written reports ultimately filled seventy-one volumes, comprising the first continuous documents about the lake and the New World. "It is a sight to arouse pity to see poor Frenchmen in a Canoe, amid rain and snow, borne hither and thither by whirlwinds in these great Lakes, which often show waves as high as those of the Sea," one Jesuit observed, adding that sometimes the weather was so bad that "the one steering the Canoe could not see his companion in the bow." He concluded, "Verily as often as they reached the land, their doing so seemed a little miracle."

After the French rule had passed, the Crown entered Superior and Englishmen, too, came to sample the big sea's weather. "We encamped . . . by moonlight on a small island," James Evans, a Wesleyan missionary, wrote in his diary while he explored Superior by canoe in October 1838 with two Indian paddlers. "On awakening in the morning, we had only to look under our blankets and eat whortleberries (blueberries), the ground being blue with them." There had been a "fine moon, mountains and limpid waters."

But the next day the missionary and his crew encountered seas that broke over their canoe; to stay afloat they bailed water all the way. "At last I turned to run for shore and risk all in running through the breakers before the wind," Evans records. They made the shelter of a small bay, but they ran their canoe over a reef of rocks, "where the heavy swells broke in angry surf." That night they barricaded themselves under their canoe and evergreen branches, listening to the roar of the lake and the howling wind. And quite probably, they prayed.

My own interest in the big lake began as a schoolboy when I read Henry Wadsworth Longfellow's famous poem, "The Song of Hiawatha."

> By the shore of Gitche Gumee,
> By the shining Big-Sea-Water.
> Stood the wigwam of Nokomis;
> Dark behind it rose the forest,
> Rose the black and gloomy pine-trees,
> Rose the firs with cones upon them;
> Bright before it beat the water,
> Beat the clear and sunny water,
> Beat the shining Big-Sea-Water.

The "shining Big-Sea-Water" was, of course, Superior. But only in recent years had I learned that there actually had been a "Hiawatha" on the lake. The poet had taken the Chippewa's god, Nanabazhoo, and had given him the name, "Hiawatha." It is said Nanabazhoo's body is entombed on an island on the big lake, and his form can still be seen in the Sleeping Giant guarding Thunder Bay.

As a young man, I had lived upon Superior's shore for nearly three years and had spent one glorious summer in a converted boathouse perched above the lake on the north shore. It was here that I had come to my true love of the lake. I remember my own special farewell when I had to leave.

It was sunset, and far off in the purple twilight an ore carrier slowly glided into the curve of the lake. A seagull wheeled above me in a tight circle, emitting a shrill cry. Waves surged toward shore in a gentle rhythm.

As darkness came, the night was filled with magic. The stars were shining pinpoints of light above a blue sea. A gentle breeze pushed lightly against me. Finally, I stood and drew a deep breath and held it as long as I could. Then I turned to leave.

It had taken me nearly a quarter of a century to return. I was older; patches of white now marked my temples. I had watched from afar as pollution, population pressure, and neglect had taken its toll on the lake. I wondered how much of the Superior I had known and loved was left—and what I would find during my lone voyage.

4

MADELINE: ENCHANTED ISLAND

MY BOW WAS LIFTING WITH THE WAVES, SMASHING OUT sheets of spray. The high winds of last night, coupled with today's 40-knot breezes, had kicked up steep wave trains. I was sailing right into them.

I sat back in the cockpit, one hand on the tiller, the other bracing myself. Despite all the bucking, I felt exhilarated and secure. The bow would rise as each wave sliced toward us. We'd climb over with a splash, and then—*whump!*—the stern would fly in the air. It was like being on a teeter-totter.

Today was the Fourth of July—the nation's Independence Day and also mine. I was at last on my odyssey on the great lake. Madeline Island lay ahead.

Only hours ago, back in Bayfield, my family had gathered to see me and *Persistence* off.

Bill had been pensive. "It'll be the first Fourth of July that we aren't together as a family."

"We were together all summer," I said. "And besides, we're enjoying the Fourth now."

"But we'll miss the fireworks together," he said.

He was right, of course, and I had no good answer.

"Good-bye," Loris said, giving me a hug and a kiss, and quickly adding, "Don't forget our radio schedule."

My son came forward with his hand outstretched, but I hugged him anyway.

"Take care of your mom," I said.

We walked to the car, and, as they began their long trip home, I waved with more vigor than I felt.

"Love you," I had called. They waved back cheerfully and dutifully. I stood there for a few minutes, feeling very alone.

Then I shoved off, sailed past the harbor entryway into the stiff chop, and turned on my course. Slowly, the sailing, the water, and the boat started to work their magic. My mood began to lift.

As we flew toward Madeline Island, I watched a few white sails in the distance—other sailors out enjoying a holiday. The large Madeline Island ferry emerged from the main dock, jammed with tourists and cars. Happy people waved at me, probably wondering what I was doing out here in such a small wooden boat. I waved back, content with my own choice of transportation.

When you sail slowly, a wonderful evolution occurs: The mind also seems to slow down and you become more and more aware of the world around you. You delight in small things—the feel of the wind, the bounding of the boat, and the sizzle of the water under the bow.

I began to relax. It would be a grand adventure after all.

I headed into the wind to drop my mainsail and to furl my jib as I came near the island. Moments later, with the engine fired up, I was edging my way toward land.

Someone standing atop a hill in what looked like a cemetery was waving a white hat at me. I could see grave markers.

I waved back.

"This way," the man shouted, pointing toward the inner harbor. I later learned he was Bill Peet, former commodore of the Madeline Island Yacht Club. The cemetery was an ancient Chippewa burial ground.

I cruised through the channel, past the graveyard, and into the nearby harbor. In minutes I had landed on one of the most unusual islands in America.

Madeline is the only island on Superior that is inhabited year-round, so I expected its natives to be particularly hardy. Although 3,000 residents come in the summer to live in large houses and play on the specially designed golf course, there are only 153 people who live full time on the island—through storms that roar in the fall and through icebound winters, when the big lake freezes and isolates them.

Nori Newago had spent most of her life on the island and was chairman of Madeline's only town, La Pointe. I liked her the moment I met her. A small, energetic woman, with blonde hair and clear eyes, Nori was married to Joe Newago, one of the last of the Chippewa on the island. Today she was behind the wheel of her car, driving us about on a sunny day with pleasant breezes.

"Sometimes we feel like we are still pioneers, challenged all of the time," Nori explained. "Everything we do is dictated by Superior. You have to respect it and you can't take chances. Nearly everyone on the island has had someone who died on the lake—my mother was drowned on it."

She stopped the car. "Here was the site of one of the first French forts on the island," she said. I walked onto the wind-swept sandy beach; ahead of me lay a sparkling vista of water with the mainland across the bay, and behind me, a thick forest. I tried to imagine the French garrison as it once was, hundreds of years ago.

Nori told me about the history of Madeline and the nearby bay. Madeline had been under three flags—French, English, and American. It was from this island that much of Lake Superior had been explored. But before any white men had been the Chippewa.

"Were they always on the island?" I asked. We had stopped at the Indian graveyard I passed on my way into the harbor. It was not far from the marina where *Persistence* was now berthed.

"They came from out east at about the same time Columbus came to this continent," Nori said. "They settled on Madeline because of its location and because it gave them protection from warring tribes."

We walked to a burial site, and I looked down at a small weathered house over a grave. We stood in silence for a moment, then Nori explained, "It is the custom here to place a little house over the grave to protect it."

"How did the Chippewa get here? By canoe?"

"Joe's grandmother recalled that there once had been a spit of sand connecting the mainland with the island. They could have just walked across on good days."

I looked at the nearby bay. On a summer day such as this, it was not hard to imagine the endless forests with magnificent trees growing down to water's edge, the lofty hill with their greens, all above the blue lake. Hiawatha land.

"Must have been idyllic," I said.

"Probably at first," Nori said, "but there were far too many people on this small island, probably as many as ten thousand, and they began to die of starvation. Then something terrible happened. It is said they turned to cannibalism and the medicine men began eating children. The tribe was horrified and eventually killed their spiritual leaders. Madeline became haunted. The tribe could hear the spirits of the dead walking the island at night; they saw globes of fire dancing on the marshes. Everyone became afraid. And that is why the Chippewa left the island and did not return for about two hundred years.

"Even then," Nori said, "and for many years after, none of the tribe liked to spend an evening on the island."

The road twisted up over a hill, away from the bay, deep into the 14-mile-long island. The woods closed in so tightly we seemed to be rushing along in a tunnel. Then we were on an open dirt road, heading toward a small cabin nestled beside a wood-covered mound.

Off to one side, not far from an open shed, I could see animal pelts stretched on frames to dry. A deer skull with antlers was suspended in a tree; I had the distinct feeling I had stepped back in time perhaps one hundred years to an early trapper's cabin. But I knew this was the home of The Digger, a man who knew more about the island's history than anyone.

A white-haired man, looking much like an oversized woods gnome dressed in weathered green shirt and pants, opened the doorway, blinking somewhat shyly in the sunlight.

"Come in, come in," Al Galazen said in a soft voice. As I entered I looked around the small area that was the living room of the cabin. On the walls hung a collection worthy of a museum, artifacts from the earliest days of America: flint arrowheads, axes and knives of stone, birchbark weavings, pieces of rusted French muskets, and small, personal ornaments from the Chippewa, the French, the English, and the early American settlers.

"My wallpaper," he explained with a motion of his hands. "I dug it up, and I dig whenever I get a chance. And that is just about every day."

The Digger began rummaging through various drawers, boxes, and cabinets. Out came rusted revolvers, knives, belt buckles, and buttons from French and English uniforms. Hundreds of years of island history were in his hands. I asked the obvious question: "How do you know where to dig?"

"The earth tells me," he said with an impish grin. "I learned the trick from an old gravedigger. This is how you find old graves. I take my long rod and I insert it in the earth. I can tell a lot by how it feels, whether the earth has been disturbed or not."

I wondered how far back he could "feel" the earth.

"For as much as a thousand years," he said proudly. "If my rod squeaks, the earth has not been disturbed."

"How do you find places to dig?"

"You have to look closely . . . a compression in the earth, something in the woods that's the wrong size, or even rocks out of place. That's the place to go. And I'm going to have some surprises for the archaeologists one of these days. Too early to talk about it, but at the other end of the island I've found traces of a very old civilization, which nobody knows existed before. Very primitive. They didn't use metal of any kind, didn't have flints, and they carried fire pots with them. They were genuine Stone Age."

"Any idea who they were?"

"The Huron. I found three thousand pieces of their material that I checked out in Canada. The island here was the end of the trail for them, they were so few." He shook his head sadly. "But there are lots of things still around on the island. I've been digging for forty years. I think I was born that way."

He began to reminisce as he rocked in his old wooden chair, and I sat down on an ancient davenport, under some of the artifacts on the wall. "I was born in 1903 in Superior, and I came to the islands over fifty years ago. I figured if it was good enough for the fish, it was good enough for me.

"When I feel like it, I just get my rod and disappear for a while. Sometimes I dig in the earth, watching for the color of the dirt as I dig. When it turns black, I start digging carefully. That's ashes from an old campfire.

"Sometimes I put waders on and dig underwater. Since about the year 1400, the island has changed a lot and some of the old campsites are underwater at Grant's Point. So long as you can see the black stuff coming up, you know you're on an old campground. I find a lot of pottery that way and rolls of birchbark. Indians and Voyageurs used birchbark to repair the skin of their canoes. They used to cook in it, too.

"I found war paint once, gray and red color in birchbark

containers. It's made out of roots, stone, and bear grease. You put it on your fingers today and you can hardly get it off. It's still good after a hundred and fifty years."

He sat still in his rocker, then poked around in an old box he had pulled from under a dresser.

"And here's my watchman!" He withdrew a human skull.

"See here?" he asked, holding up the skull for me to admire. "I dug him up. That's a bullet hole. I date the skull from the late 1700s, and from the uniform remains, he was a British soldier. I'd guess his age to be about thirty-five."

"He's your watchman?" I asked, taking the offered skull.

"Whenever I go away, I just put him out in the middle of the floor. If anybody breaks in here, especially at night, they'll see my watchman and get scared off."

"Does it work?"

"Nobody's taken anything yet!"

Here and there a few tourists lazed along the island's main street, and a few cars passed. It was hard to think of La Pointe as having a downtown; mostly it was a collection of one- and two-story frame buildings of indeterminate age and construction, rising to what seemed to be the focal point—Nelson's grocery, a gas station, a restaurant, and a bar.

I was wondering what to do next when I saw the island's patrol car, so I waved at it. The patrolman slowed his car, then rolled down his window.

"My name's Marlin Bree," I said. "I'd like to talk with you."

"Okay," he said, but I knew he was suspicious.

"I sailed in yesterday. I've got that wooden sailboat in Three-C."

"The little varnished one?"

"Right. I spent seven years building it and I'm sailing Superior this summer. Can I ride with you for a while?"

He shrugged his shoulders and said, "Hop in." Patrolman Jim Cook was a stout-looking young man. As he drove, he told me that patrolling the island from tip to tip over all its roads, a distance of fifty-two miles in all, "usually takes less than two hours without hurrying."

"How long does it take to drive through downtown?" I asked.

"About two minutes," he said, with all seriousness. "But I haven't been bored yet, and I've been here since September."

Cook was a sportsman and a naturalist, which must have drawn him here. "The island supports a population of deer that was once quite heavy, but because of bad winters and hunting pressures, they thinned out. Now they're coming back. In the course of my patrols, if I don't see three or four deer, I'll consider that a very slow night.

"I even see deer downtown. They cross the town to get to the harbor to drink. We've got a big herd behind town hall, and at one time I could count fifteen.

"Last Sunday I saw a deer die on Grant's Point. It was a nice buck, in heavy sand. It was in convulsions and died before we could do anything. Hard to say what happened, but it could have been run to death by dogs or coyotes. We get quite a lot of that out here."

"Any wolves on the island?" I asked. I knew that the last pack of this endangered species lived on Superior's shores.

"No wolves," he said. "We have feral dogs in abundance—dogs that have gone back to the wild to live. And there are a lot of coyote-dog crosses, sometimes with unusual results. I once saw a pure white coyote. I was patrolling the island airport, and the first thing I noticed was bushy tail and ears, and despite the color, it was sure enough a coyote."

A speeding car roared by and Patrolman Cook stamped hard on the accelerator. "Speeder," he said. "Excuse me." Red light flashing atop the patrol car, we rocketed ahead. Moments later, the offending car pulled meekly to the side of the road. Cook got out, adjusting his pistol in its holster, then, a few minutes later, he returned smiling. "That was the best excuse I heard all week. He said he was trying to beat the rain—to get his tent closed up."

I laughed. "What did you do?"

"Well, I just told him on the island we like to keep the speed down."

"What about crime on the island?" I asked. "I notice that the islanders don't lock their doors when they go out."

"Think about it. This is an island. What can you steal large enough to make you money that you can carry across on the ferry? Once there were some motorcycle gangs up from the Cities and they were ready for trouble. I had to tell them not to hit me for their own good."

"Did that work?"

"They got the message. They realized they were isolated here. There's nowhere to go that they can't be found. So where can they run?"

We were now completing the sweep of the island to the north and heading along the eastern shore. Off past the shoreline lay Chequamegon Bay, and through the trees I could see a two-story white house with a large, grassy knoll leading up from the lake.

Sticking out from a tall bush, near some trees, was what looked like the tail of a small aircraft. I blinked, then looked again in disbelief. It really was an airplane. As the patrol car drew nearer, I could see wings. Atop the plane, the American flag flew proudly. It looked like a World War I fighter that had crashed.

"Oh, that," Patrolman Cook said with a nonchalant gesture of his thumb. "That's the Red Baron's plane."

"I must meet him sometime."

"Hurry," came the reply. "He takes an awful lot of chances."

My next stop was at the office of the *Island Gazette* ($5 a year, circulation 600, no advertising). Its editor, Sally Burke, had been born in the islands, spent much of her time as a fisherman's wife, and was now a widow in her mid-fifties. Her white-flecked hair was neatly tied in two braids, which in turn were coiled around her head. She was working on the newspaper's winter issue, which included a photo page about ice. I began to think of the isolation of the island, when the big lake was frozen, and the unusual "ice road" that connected the island to the mainland. Sally told me this season two cars had plunged to the bottom.

"Why'd they go through?"

"One car didn't stay on the ice trail and another one decided to take a shortcut and came too close to shore," she said, adding that one car was a—she paused for proper disparaging emphasis—"a Cadillac." I decided that perhaps some islanders, notably Sally, didn't like luxury cars. "We're good at fishing out Cadillacs here," she said with a knowing smile. "But if you talk to Arnie or Wayne, the Nelson boys, who go out on the ice every day, they'd tell you where it was safe."

Arnie Nelson, she told me, was in charge of the island's ice sled, which gets across when the ice isn't heavy enough to bear the weight of cars; his brother, Wayne, was in charge of the ice road. It was Wayne's job to go out alone in his pickup truck each day to check the "road," mark the route if there are any cracks or weak places, and report back to the islanders. Implicit here, I gathered, was that if he made it back, the road was safe.

"If it's too cold, the ice can get brittle," Sally said. "One car may get across, but it may create a crack for another car to break through. On the ice, it's definitely best not to be second. And you never know if somebody has gone an hour ahead of you.

"Usually there is plenty of time before you're in trouble so you can get out—a wheel goes in and then the car gradually settles. If you are on real bad ice, though, there is no time—the car tips and the weight pulls it down. I remember once I was on two solid feet of ice in a GMC pickup going to Bayfield for beer, but the temperature dropped. A heavy load had just gone across, a crack had formed, and some-

body didn't know it or didn't mark it. Our truck went onto
the cake and began sliding into the water. I opened the door
to get out, and that was scary. If I had gotten off on the
wrong side, I wouldn't be here today."

She paused for a moment. "But whether it's frozen or
liquid, everybody who goes out on the lake gets caught
sooner or later," she said and seemed to look hard at me.
"My grandfather lost his life sailing from Bayfield carrying the mail. He tried going across in April, when the ice
was moving out, but the ice moved back in and capsized his
little boat."

I changed the subject. "You were a fisherwoman at one
time. Did you ever get caught?"

"Once we were in our boat on the north end of the island.
The day was so still that not a leaf was blowing. But as we
came around Steamboat Point, we ran right into a vicious
storm. I was steering, and when my husband came back to
the wheelhouse, his face had turned white. He took the
wheel from me, but our boat was old and a little punky in
the stern, and he was afraid to turn and run. So he decided
to face the storm. We must have had seventy-mile-an-hour
winds and some of the waves were higher than our boat.
There was no reason looking for life preservers, because
you're better off remaining with the boat. It would probably stay up long enough to land somewhere, with you in it.
We had a rough time, but eventually we made it back."

However, her boat didn't survive all of Superior's storms.
"She was built in 'Thirty-nine, but went down in 'Forty-
nine," Sally said. *Dawn* had sunk at anchor. A southwester
had come in too fast and seas had broken in the gangway.
"She went underwater for two miles, then came up on a
sandy beach. She was missing her superstructure and one
whole side.

"They told my husband that she was done for. But the
Dawn was his life and he wouldn't give her up. So he began
working on her, despite everyone's advice. And in a while,
she was back fishing for another thirty years."

It was only a fifteen-minute ride along a bumpy gravel road in Sally's old car. And there was the *Dawn,* perched jauntily in a green meadow behind some pine trees.

"The kids put on a coat of paint now and then," Sally said, "to try to keep her up."

She walked to *Dawn*'s side and ran her hand along the planking. "She looks like hell now. But once she was nice." Then Sally patted the little boat. "I think I'll just keep her right here. I figure she deserves a good resting place."

Near the middle of the island, at the center of a sand excavation pit, stood a rusty steel-covered building. Arnie Nelson and I drove down and entered.

"Well . . . there she is," Arnie said, partly pulling back the covering. The large machine hulking under a dusty tarpaulin looked like it could have landed from outer space. But the longer I stared, the more it resembled a boat—one with runners and powered by what looked like a huge aircraft engine. It was, I knew, the island's ice sled.

"This is our third sled," Arnie said, showing me its features. "First, we had a wooden one, but that lasted only five years. It got wood fatigue from all the bending and twisting of getting in and out of the water. This aluminum one twists also, but when it cracks, you just weld it back up."

The islanders had taken a 250-horsepower army surplus tank engine, vintage about 1946, and mounted it in the rear of the craft to swing a wooden propeller. The driver's seat and controls were up front. The 20-foot-long hull was made of ⅜-inch-thick aluminum and rode on 6-inch-wide runners with stainless steel over them. Protruding out front, raised and lowered by a hydraulic jack, was an ungainly-looking tire used to help the machine get on and off the ice. The machine wouldn't win any beauty prizes.

"You steer with rudders in the back. The ride is rough and nasty, but very fast. And it's not easy to learn how to drive. Wind is a big factor—it likes to go sideways in the wind. The solution is more power and more rudder. But when you do that, you go faster."

I wondered how he had learned to handle this beast. He smiled. "The first time I learned to drive was by getting in and going to Bayfield to pick up people."

"What's it like on a crossing?"

"Every trip is different, whether you're in deep snow, glare ice, or channel ice. Open water is the smoothest, but the passengers don't like it because we don't mind plunging right in. If people see the open water coming up, we try to give them a little encouragement to let them know this thing floats. I have had some people try to pay me double if I'd go slower. But I can't because we have a schedule to keep. Besides, it's cold out there.

"Mostly it's routine. We haul the school kids, passengers and mail, and everything we need on the island. The average crossing is about thirty miles per hour. That's on the ice and in and out of the water. But on glare ice, our speed builds up fast. I've had it over a hundred miles per hour, and at a hundred it's a little scary.

"Sometimes we use it for rescue. We've gone out to fishermen caught in the ice packs and we have been down to Prairie du Chien, in Wisconsin, when we were hired by the hospital to haul doctors, nurses, and patients across the Mississippi. The bridge was out, and we roared back and forth around the clock. The rescues we don't like are when someone falls through the ice up here. There was a snowmobiler who was last seen on thin ice, and we couldn't find anything beyond where the tracks ended. We searched and divers went down under the ice, and there he was, in seventy feet of water right by his snowmobile. He must have had a heart attack."

He leaned back in the July sun. "People rely on us and it's our hobby to pick people up off the ice. You could call this more or less of a service, but it's really part of the island. Our fees barely pay for maintenance, and"—he seemed almost philosophical—"if we broke down, who'd come to get us?"

Without pausing for an answer, he turned around and walked back to his car.

It had fabric on the wings and tail—the rest was exposed aluminum tubing. The wing was high, and on top was a strut with wires, much like old-fashioned biplane bracing. Its engine, a modified snowmobile motor, was in back; and in front of the wing, nearly on the ground, was the pilot's seat.

"I just run it into the bushes to keep the wind off it," the Red Baron explained, now giving the plane an affectionate push backward. His Rally Sport ultralight, *Beauford T.*, came out obediently, its red wings shining brightly. It seemed to shiver in the Superior breezes.

Wayne Nelson, alias the Red Baron of Madeline Island, was an intense man in his late twenties or early thirties. Despite the chill air, he wore a light shirt, jeans, and tattered sneakers. He seemed constantly to be moving about, his dark eyes darting everywhere.

He sniffed the air like a sailor, then felt it on his face. "It's a little breezy today, gusting up to about thirty-five knots, but I was brought up with winds forty-five to fifty knots. Up here, if you want to fly, you fly.

"I've been flying planes since I was old enough to sit on my dad's lap, so I've spent a lot of time in the air. I love flying. But more than that, it's one of the salvations of my sanity. When the world gets to be too much for me, I go up in the sky."

I had heard stories of him and his airplane—and seagulls.

"Someone's been talking," the Baron said, suspiciously. "It's true that I catch seagulls," he admitted, then explained. "Ducks are much too fast and so are cormorants. But seagulls fly at about forty-five miles per hour, and that's

about right for me and *Beauford T.* You come up from behind them as they fly along. When you get within fifty feet,
they'll start getting nervous and turn their heads, and
you'll see these black eyes on you, wondering what you are
going to do. Oh, they'll try a fake maneuver, trying to throw
you off, because they're smart birds. But once they discover
you're as smart as they are, the duel begins in earnest."

His arms outstretched wide, he began to imitate flight
patterns of the seagull as he explained.

"So they'll keep turning their heads around, watching
you, because they figure you're another bird. So when they
see you lift one wing they'll figure you're going one way,
and they'll immediately head the other way." With his arms
upswept, the Baron swung down and around.

"So what you do is you fake them out with a quick little
wing lift," he said, shifting his arms. "When they turn the
other way, you turn with them on the inside—then you've
got them!" He stood upright now, his eyes gleaming.

"You catch them? With your hands?"

"Oh, no! Nothing like that. That might hurt the bird,"
the Baron said. "What you do is you touch wings with them,
and just *kind* of catch them. Doesn't hurt them at all, except for one thing. Their tail feathers go out and up; it's
undignified and they look silly. It hurts their pride."

"Then?"

"Oh, I hold them there on my wing for a few seconds,
then edge off my throttle, and off they fly." He grinned.
"My dog likes that, too."

"You take your dog up in your ultralight?" His dog was
part wolf, already weighed over 100 pounds, and was not
yet fully grown.

"You can if you tuck him in between your legs. Just his
head sticks out. He loves it!"

I imagined the two of them, the young flyer and the wolf-
hound with his ears flapping in the breeze, sailing over the
islands. But I was surprised to learn he flew year-round,

both because he was in charge of the ice road and as well as for fun.

"It's really not awfully cold up there," he explained. "An ultralight only goes thirty-four to forty miles per hour, and because *Beauford T.* has a pod, the wind goes around you. I wear a ski mask, full helmet, chopper gloves, and a snowmobile suit.

"Actually, a little airplane like this is very handy in winter. I can fly out over the ice and check its condition, look for lost snowmobilers, for cars that have broken through the ice—all sorts of things."

Just months before, in dead of winter, the Coast Guard had called the Baron at about midnight. A fishing boat from Red Cliff, the *Energy*, had been caught beside Devil's Island—the outermost of the Apostles—in an ice jam-up. Could he help?

The next morning, he flew to the Bayfield Coast Guard station and landed his plane on the ice. But he was told his volunteer services were no longer needed—they had called in a jet fighter to the rescue.

The Baron shook his head. "I decided to go out for myself and take a look. As I arrived over the island, I saw a Coast Guard jet throttle back to a hundred and fifty miles an hour, trying to assess the problem, but at that speed, obviously, he couldn't see much. Off in the distance, too, I could see the *Sundew*, the large Coast Guard boat out of Duluth."

"What did you do?"

"The ice was too rough for me to land on the frozen lake, so I found myself a landing place on Devil's Island. I came in over a fifty-foot cliff, landed, and walked as near as I could to the boat."

From his cliffside vantage point, the Baron could talk with the *Energy*'s captain, Cecil Peterson. His crew and he had been fishing when the ice moved in, shoving the 40-foot boat up in the air 20 feet. There it perched, heeled over dangerously.

I could imagine the harried skipper seeing this tiny airplane buzzing over him, landing atop a cliff where an airplane really shouldn't be able to land—then the pilot popping out to see if *he* could be of any help.

"The captain was surprised," the Baron said. "He told me his crew and he were all right, but that they were really hungry. I had seen some fishermen on my way out by North Twin Island. I turned *Beauford T.* around, took off, and landed on the ice by the fishermen and explained Cecil's problem. They gave me three great big whitefish, and I dropped them down on the deck of the *Energy*.

"Then I went back to Madeline and talked with my brother; Arnie decided to put supplies in the ice sled and go out to the *Energy*. But I told him there was an ice maize going in, with ridges up to twelve feet high. Part of the way was glare ice, part was open water.

"The problem with the ice sled is that the only way to steer it is with power. But more power also means you are going faster, with less maneuverability, and there are no brakes. So it got down to this: How could Arnie keep the sled going fast enough to maneuver, yet wind through the maize of ice ridges? I decided to scout ahead in *Beauford T.*, with Arnie coming down the ice after me in the sled.

"I'd fly along an expansion ridge and when I found a place where the ice sled could cross, I'd land and turn my plane around to show the right direction. Then, without slowing down, he'd roar by my nose.

"Finally, after fifty or sixty takeoffs and landings, I had Arnie alongside the stranded fishing boat. I landed atop Devil's Island again and walked to the edge, then got onto the ice floe, just in time to hear Arnie's first words."

" 'Dr. Livingston, I presume . . .'? " I joked.

"No. Arnie looked up at the surprised crew and asked, 'You ordered pizza?'

"The situation was serious, though, and Arnie is an ice expert. The *Sundew* wanted the men off the boat, but Cecil and his crew refused to leave because the boat was their life. The *Sundew* didn't want to get too close, either, because the *Energy* could capsize.

"Arnie swung back and forth along the ice ridge to examine the condition of the ice. The ridge was composed of individual cakes of ice, and if pressure could be brought at a certain point, it would collapse.

"The *Sundew* nudged its steel bow into the ice; the ridge collapsed like a log pile. Down slid the *Energy,* right into the water. The whole operation took an hour and a half, maybe two."

Out on the lake, past the cliff, the wind was whipping up whitecaps. "A northeaster," he said. "It's the weirdest wind. Cold, so the plane will fly better, but with lots of down draft, so you always seem to lose a couple of hundred feet."

We pushed the small aircraft to the center of the grassy strip he called his airfield. The engine coughed into life, then settled into a healthy snarl. The Baron sank down into his seat just inches above the grass.

He gave me the thumbs-up signal, as if he were a World War I ace, and taxied to the edge of the cliff. Suddenly, he spun about, facing up the hill toward the row of dark pines. He paused for a moment, as if timing the wind blast, then roared in my direction.

The red aircraft skimmed across the grass up the hill, passing under a power line. The engine screamed. When it was nearly abreast of me, it snapped into the air, climbing at a high angle, to rise toward the tall pines at the edge of the airfield. He cleared the treetops with only feet to spare.

Suddenly, the tiny airplane seemed to be shoved sideways. Northeaster! The Red Baron swung outward, righted himself, and headed into the wind. He seemed to hang motionless in the gale, like a kite on a string. But then he turned, and another blast seemed to carry him rapidly out toward the open lake. I lost sight of him.

I ran toward the edge of the cliff. This was where he would return—and he did, blowing in out of the blue sky with the northeaster. Down, down he came, barely skimming the cliff, and with a soft plop, landed on the grass. Almost reverently, he pushed his aircraft back to its shelter behind the bushes.

There was a question I needed to ask him. I paused a moment. "Don't you ever worry?"

The Baron looked thoughtful, his dark eyes glittered. "Anyone who tells you he isn't afraid sometimes when he's flying or sailing is either stupid or a fool," he said, finally. "Fear is always there and that is not important. It's what you do with it that is. At times I feel like there are two of me. One person is saying, 'Stay back,' and the other is telling me, 'Meet the challenge.' I have been afraid many times. I don't see fear as the end of anything—it's merely a barrier to get across."

Bill Peet parked his car by a path leading into the dark pine woods. The Old Commodore and I ambled down the rutty trail, which was partly covered with bogs of water, sidestepping low-lying branches. We were on our way to see the legendary sailor, Rufus Jefferson.

"Is that his real name, Rufus C. Jefferson?" I asked.

"Oh, yes. His daddy was a captain and quite a joker. And don't be surprised by his boat. He designs and builds his own. It's how he believes a Lake Superior boat should be."

"The Baron told me he sees Rufus in a rowboat out on Superior just watching his model boats sail."

"That's right. He loves to build and test model boats of his own design. That's how he arrived at his twenty-footer."

"That's the size of *my* boat!"

"But his is altogether different. It's about as cobby a boat as you'll ever see; it's rough as hell. Rufus doesn't believe in fancy, he only believes in strong. It is about as massive a boat for its size as you can find."

"Heavy displacement? It sounds slow."

"Oh, no. Let me tell you about our first Madeline Island to Isle Royale race. Rufus doesn't want anything to do with being called a yachtsman, so officially he was not entered in our race. But there he was anyway at the starting line. He claimed he was just going out 'cruising' in the same direction we were.

"Well, he didn't fool anybody. Just as the race neared Rock of Ages reef on Isle Royale, Rufus's little twenty-footer was one of the first boats there. But Lake Superior got to be Lake Superior, and when we got back to Madeline, there was no sign of Rufus.

"I got worried, so I hired an airplane to look for him or the wreckage of his boat. Eventually, my search circle extended far enough so that I found him on the other side of the lake. There he was, he and his little boat, just sailing along. And when I finally talked to him on the radio, he had the audacity to claim he had finished cruising, and just wanted to do a little real sailing. I got mad."

"What did you do?"

"We decided to send him the bill for the plane charter, but he never paid. Sometime later, he showed up with a model boat which he had constructed."

"And?"

"We accepted, of course. It was a beautiful boat."

"Maybe that was all he could pay."

"Not Rufus. He just doesn't believe in spending money unnecessarily."

I laughed. The Old Commodore shook his head. "No, it's true. Rufus just believes in simplifying his life as much as possible, and if he does not have to spend money, he won't."

"Are his boats cheaply built?"

"Oh, no. Rufus builds in the finest materials that will do the job, but he will look hard before he'll spend money. His woods are local for his keel and his ribs, and for clenching nails he imports some zinc-plated steel from the Orient."

I thought back to my own building program for the *Persistence*. Though she was covered with 6-ounce fiberglass on the bottom, plus epoxy graphite, and 4-ounce glass wrapped everywhere else, leaving literally no place for water to get to the wood, I had used the finest in woods. I had fastened using epoxy glue along with expensive silicone bronze or stainless steel screws or bolts. I was surprised that any builder of integrity—which obviously Rufus was—would use Hong Kong nails.

"Everything on that boat of his works," the Old Commodore said. "He's had that little boat for over twenty years and he's sailed it all around the lake. He doesn't keep it at a dock. He just has a mooring out in Superior, and he chains it to that. It's exposed to every storm that comes along."

I shook my head. "Tell me if it's true that he only goes sailing when it storms."

"Oh, it's probably true," he said, shrugging his shoulders. "You know, that's when it's the most fun."

"Even during a northeaster?"

"Yes. But you have to have rock-solid confidence in your boat. You have to feel that even if it rolls over twice, on the third roll it will come upright."

"When Rufus comes across a northeaster, what does he do?"

"He claims he gets bored, and he 'heaves to,' so the boat can steer itself slowly, then he goes below for a nap." Peet indulged himself in a wry grin. "He must get a lot of sleep."

We walked through heavy woods, then suddenly came upon a sun-drenched grassy knoll overlooking the lake. I saw a two-story frame house with many windows and, partly tucked into the woods, a large newly built shed.

Rufus was inside the boathouse working on a 28-foot sailboat. He was clench-nailing planking to steamed oak framing, one nail per join. The boat itself looked like it was all keel, massively built and a throwback to an 1880 displacement Pilot boat. But I knew it had to be one of Rufus's own designs.

Rufus was in khakis, his shirtsleeves rolled up over his elbows. He was medium in size, with closely cropped steel-gray hair, but his arms were massive. His blue eyes were surrounded by crow's-feet and looked as if he had squinted over many oceans.

"How are the Hong Kong nails working out?" the Old Commodore probed.

Rufus stiffened almost imperceptibly. "Just fine. You know, I have galvanized fastenings on my twenty-footer, and they've held up okay."

"True enough," Bill grudgingly admitted.

"So why pay more?" Rufus pressed his point.

"Just out of curiosity," I asked, "have you looked at the new construction techniques, such as epoxy-glued wood?"

Rufus sniffed in disdain. "It's not a natural for a boat. The old-timers knew how to build good boats and I've had success with their proven techniques." Then he added, "Besides, epoxy costs too much.

"You know my twenty-footer? I keep it chained to a mooring on the lake. There are times when I look out in a storm and all I can see is the mast sticking out."

"How do you come in during rough weather?" I asked.

"Carefully," he said. "You really get only one chance to grab your mooring as you come in. Especially during a northeaster."

"Let me do a couple of fastenings, then we'll go in the house," Rufus said. I picked up a heavy hammer and placed its head on the steam-bent frame. He began hammering a clench nail through the plank. I could feel the force of the blow on the shivering wood. In a few strokes, the heavy nail came through the Port Orford cedar and oak and struck my hammer, its tip folded over. The plank and frame were now married together by the nail—the old-fashioned way to build a boat. It looked strong.

"Goes easy enough," Rufus said, pleased. "And I don't use glues, either."

We walked up the hill into the house. "No electricity, no telephones," Rufus said.

The living room was airy and filled with light from windows overlooking the lake. On the wood-planked walls were kerosene ship's lanterns and in one corner was a beautiful hand-carved church organ. A ladder with a rope handrail led up to a second-floor loft. Everywhere, on display and in handmade boxes, were ship's models.

"Good to have you back on the island," the Old Commodore said. "How long will you be here?"

"March."

He had just arrived from Minneapolis and planned to winter on the island—total time of about nine months devoted to boatbuilding. I envied him.

"What else have you been up to?" the Old Commodore asked.

"I've been in the Falkland Islands. They've become a graveyard of the last of the great sailing ships. You know, some of the clippers. I want to study them and bring one of them back if possible," Rufus said. "They're part of our sailing heritage.

"But you have to see my boat now," Rufus said, changing the subject. "It has been stored all winter but I'll bet that my diesel will still start on the first pull-through."

I walked to the shed, and there was his boat, a double-ender, beamy in the extreme and all keel—like old-fashioned boats. The Old Commodore was right: She was as cobby-looking a twenty-foot boat as I'd ever seen. She had a bowsprit and a wooden tabernacle, and though I didn't examine the wooden mast up close, I was certain the sails would be set on hoops or tied on. Again, the old-fashioned way.

"Look, no fancy cockpit," Rufus said, swinging up and aboard. "Just big enough to stand in, and you can steer by leaning against the tiller." He demonstrated by putting the massive stub of a tiller against his back and moving the rudder with his body. "Nothing fancy, just very simple and strong. Nothing to fail.

"I've sailed this boat everywhere on Superior. It has never let me down. But I'll give you a suggestion: If you are sailing alone, trail a line in the water. Twice I fell over-board, and the only thing that saved me was that line. I grabbed it and pulled myself back on board. Otherwise I just would have watched my boat sail off without me."

He went below. "Now watch this." I heard him turning something over, and with a cough of black smoke, his diesel came to life. "See? Everything works," he said, as the diesel chugged away after having been stored all winter.

"You'll have a grand time sailing Superior," he said. "But be careful of northeasters, especially on the north shore. That's a bad place to be."

As the Old Commodore and I walked down the wooded trail back to the car, something occurred to me. "Rufus is in terrific shape," I said, "but how old do you think he is?"

"I don't know. But you remember he showed us a picture of himself on Lake Minnetonka when he rowed himself to school. The picture was dated 1933."

"And if he was in his teens then . . ."

"That's right. He must be in his late sixties."

It was Monday morning. Once again, I had spent the night in the island marina, listening to the soft wind in the rigging, smelling the fresh air of the island, and feeling the boat gently bob in the water. Though I had already been too long on this beautiful island, I was reluctant to leave.

The day was bright and clear. I started my engine, then began moving out of the harbor onto the waters of Superior. I'd stop at Bayfield for provisions and then journey to my next port of call: the Red Cliff Reservation.

But there was one last thing to do—a last-moment in-spiration. At the breakwater, I turned to follow the shore-line, and there they were—the Old Commodore and his wife—walking on the beach, taking in the morning sun. They looked up at my approach, then pointed excitedly toward my boat. I stood up in the cockpit as I neared, and, raising my right hand to my brow, I honored them with an old-fashioned salute. It was my way of thanking him and saying good-bye to this wonderful island.

The Old Commodore's face broke into a grin of understanding. He waved back, and returned my nautical salute.

With that, I turned my bow to the west. I felt free as the wind and accountable to no one but myself.

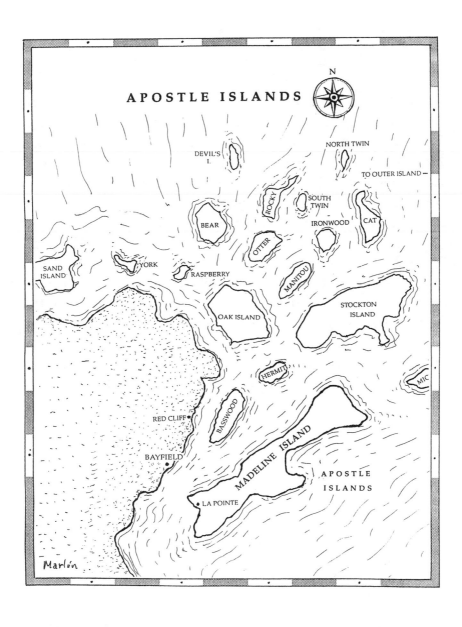

5

MOON OVER RED CLIFF

PERSISTENCE'S BOW CUT CLEANLY IN THE BLUE WATERS. It was a warm, sunny day, and I was enjoying sailing among the Apostle Islands. Off my starboard bow was the darkness of Basswood Island; far ahead I could see the sparkling green of Oak Island. Wild blueberries and raspberries grew among the tall pines that stretched from the water's edge.

Why these legendary and historic islands, jewels of green in the shining big sea, were called the Apostles has been a question for hundreds of years. One story has it that in the 1600s, French missionaries thought there were twelve islands and named them after the twelve apostles. But this doesn't seem likely; anyone voyaging in these waters, even in canoes, quickly would discover there are, in fact, twenty-two.

Another account traces the name to a band of pirates, the Twelve Apostles, that once made Basswood Island its headquarters. As fur- or trade-good-laden canoes paddled by, the pirates would sweep out to hijack cargoes.

"Red Cliff Marina . . . Red Cliff Marina. . . ." I repeated into my VHF radio. "This is the *Persistence*. Over." I called several times, but there was no answer.

I took down my sails, then entered the breakwall with my engine turning over at slow speed. The marina was small, snugged up to the overshadowing cliff, which cut off the wind. The day felt very hot, almost sultry.

A boy fishing off one of the docks barely glanced my way as I glided so near I could almost reach out and touch his line. "Where can I berth?" I asked. He shrugged in a good-humored manner, waved to a row of open berths, and went back to fishing.

Matters were not so simple for me—I was still not exactly certain where to dock. Finally, I just picked an empty spot.

Hot, tired, and long overdue for a shower, I rummaged about the cabin for a towel and my toilet gear and walked up the hill to a meandering road along the cliff's edge. It felt good to stretch my legs.

Above me rose another hill with a heavily wooded summit, and along its edge stretched a spacious, grassy campgrounds with colorful nylon tents. I walked past families starting to build fires for their evening meals. The air was fragrant with campfire smoke, pine trees, and food, and carried the sound of children laughing and playing.

These were not the Ojibway. This was a modern campgrounds they operated for tourists. The tribal members, I learned later, had settled higher up on the cliff in condominiums and modern apartments.

Refreshed after a lengthy shower, shampoo, and shave, I started back through the pines, down a steep slope to my quiet home on the water. I saw that a number of people, all with fishing poles and lines, were now on the docks of the deserted marina. Some sat on portable camp stools, others with their legs dangling over the piers; all were intent on fishing. A small community had sprung up around the boats. I later found out that it was some of the Red Cliff tribe enjoying their twilight fishing.

I walked past a man opposite my boat, feeling a little like an intruder now.

"How's fishing?" I asked.

"Good," the elderly man replied amiably, and then went back to his fishing. Not far away, a boy of about twelve held up several fish he had caught. The old man nodded his head and gave him a brief smile.

I went aboard *Persistence*, glanced at the people fishing, and decided to go ahead with my life on board the boat. Nobody seemed to notice when I placed my freshly washed laundry on stainless steel lifelines to dry.

I heard a splash and the sound of the tribe's excited laughter. Several children danced up and down at the end of the pier, pointing. I looked around, and there, in the water, was something about the size of a small dog, its nose just sticking out as it sped along.

"What is it?" I asked.

"Beaver!" someone said. We watched the animal's progress with delight. It swam for a while, then the furry creature dived under the water, disappearing about 50 feet from my boat.

Sitting in the cockpit, I watched the sun set and my first day at Red Cliff turned into a warm and kind evening. In the deepening shadows of the pines and the blues of a Superior twilight, I began to feel at home and . . .

> Heard the whispering of the pine trees,
> Heard the lapping of the water,
> Sounds of music, words of wonder.

Soon dusk turned into night, and up on the cliff, the wind sighed through the pines. Just above Basswood Island, a giant, tawn-colored moon had arisen, its light reflecting silvery on wide waters like a welcoming smile. Civilization's problems seemed far away.

The next morning dawned humid and warm, and I arose late and stretched. Sliding open my hatch, I saw someone walk rapidly to the end of the dock, squint at the waters, then shake his head.

"Have you seen the *Ranger*?" asked a wiry man in his mid-thirties. His name, I learned, was Dick Bowker.

I shook my head, but he continued: "I was supposed to meet her at nine, but I don't see her. I've repaired her jib." He walked over to *Persistence*, peering down. "Nice boat! Did you build her yourself?"

"Seven years," I said.

He told me he and his wife, Ann, were sailmakers. He scanned the waters one last time for the missing *Ranger*, then decided to return in an hour. Dick then invited me to their log cabin in the woods.

Ann was waiting in their old Volkswagen and soon we were climbing the cliff away from Superior. In just minutes, we were in deep north woods, away from the Indian reservation. The pines rose darkly against the morning sun's rosy hues.

"Originally, I was a biology teacher," Dick said, shifting to a lower gear for our steep ascent up a forested back road. "But I was deeply frustrated in the school system. I was going nowhere. One day I saw my first copy of the *Mother Earth News* and I realized we had a lot of options. Getting out was one of them. We found a piece of land that was a mile and a half from nowhere, and so we built a log cabin."

Ann turned to me, her eyes sparkling. "We made a pact. We'd stay just one year, and if either of us didn't like it, we'd leave. Two years passed and we were so happy we never got around to voting."

"We moved just before Christmas," Dick said. "Our first home was just a little tar paper shack. It was all we could do and all we could afford. We had sold nearly everything we owned just to get there. Still, it was a tremendous change to make with two young sons. We had a wood stove for heat and a wood cookstove. And we had hope."

"What did you do for money?"

"Anything that needed being done," Ann said. "And that included snow shoveling."

The Volkswagen was in first gear, grinding up a rough

trail through the woods. Dick pointed to a pond of clear water overshadowed by trees. "Our swimming and bathing pool," he said. "At the end of the day we love to jump in and relax."

"Summers only," Ann added.

We reached a cleared trail now, and I peered along a corridor of dark green pines. At the top of a grassy hill overlooking a lush woodland meadow was a cabin constructed of heavy logs. The Bowkers hadn't been exaggerating.

"It's two stories and sturdy," Dick said. "Seventeen by twenty-four on the outside and sixteen by twenty-three on the inside. We live in the downstairs and sleep upstairs."

"Walls a foot thick? Where did you get the logs?"

"From a logger, unpeeled and uncut. We went to work ourselves with broad axes, to flatten the logs on top and bottom, and raised our own home. We put some fiberglass between the logs, but basically that's the only place we used stuffing; the weight of the logs seals the walls."

Ann opened the door, motioning for me to follow. There was the faint but pleasant feeling of being inside a heavily wooded area. I smelled the slightly acid but not distasteful aroma of a hardwood fire and turned to see a large cast-iron wood stove burning in the center of the open room, where it could radiate heat all around the house. Against one wall were rows of neatly cut wood.

I had always expected to find a log house dark, but this one was full of light. There were large windows along one wall. The Bowkers had an unspoiled panorama of grassy woodland meadow framed by dark north pines.

"No curtains," I said. "Or shades?"

Dick stepped up expansively. "Look, no neighbors!"

Attached to one side of the cabin was their workshop, which was very bright. "Windows and skylights," Dick said. "You need a lot of light for our work."

He settled comfortably in front of his sewing machine. Its frame was of black metal, cast for strength, and the metallic parts gleamed brightly. It was a new industrial machine with a foot-powered treadle they had devised. As Dick rocked his foot back and forth on the treadle, the machine came alive.

"It works better than an electric one. Here, try it yourself."

I sat down at the machine and rocked my foot on the treadle. It ran effortlessly and quickly.

"It sews at about twelve hundred stitches per minute," Dick said. The teacher in him was coming out again. "An electric industrial machine runs at two thousand, but in our work, control is more important than speed. We find we don't use even our full speed; we prefer having control."

There was another reason why the foot-powered machine was desirable—they had no electricity.

"We don't need it, either," Dick said, "with one exception."

We walked to the kitchen. Dick flipped a switch, and there was light, but only a little. He pointed to a single fluorescent tube suspended from the ceiling. "It's from a boat, powered by a battery."

"Neat, but how do you keep your battery charged up?"

"The Volkswagen," he said, telling me his ingenious solution. "We have *two* batteries: one in the car and one in the house. When the kitchen light battery runs down, we put it in the car, and in the normal course of running around, it gets charged up again. In the meantime, we use the car's battery in the house."

Dick told me that they would also be adding solar and wind power, so they would not be dependent upon public power. "Living without electricity, your life ends up being whole. You don't pay for it in installments at the end of each month. By getting control of exactly what you need, you can match your expenses directly with your income. But you don't spend what you don't have and you don't buy what you don't need. We've eliminated a lot of nonessential things from our lives. We've found we can do without them. For example, when dark comes, we read a bit by kerosene lamp and then we go to bed early."

He crossed his arms in front of himself, thoughtfully. "But above all, we have created our own life-style, away from the meaningless work-eat-sleep cycle we used to have."

"A life-style that emphasizes life spirit, nature, and friends," Ann added, "is more important to us than one centered on possessions, gadgets, prestige, and power."

"Our life is very satisfying," Dick said. "And, to us, it's correct."

Now I was in the backseat of the Volkswagen and we were descending the hill to Red Cliff, again in search of the yacht, *Ranger*. I glanced out the window at the marina below.

By the edge of the pier, just past my boat, were two huge, brightly painted canoes. I had never seen boats like these.

"What are they?" I asked.

"The Voyageur canoes have returned," Dick said.

I walked rapidly down to the docks. Since childhood, I had heard tales of the original Voyageurs—the legendary northmen who traveled the wilderness in their birchbark canoes. Their prodigious strength and energy, and in particular, their remarkable spirit and ability to disregard pain and danger, still inspired me. They were the stuff of which heroes are made.

Now I looked at the modern-day Voyageurs. Some of them were still on their boats, but most were up on a hill overlooking the bay. They wore blue jeans and T-shirts and some sported brightly colored nylon jackets. They looked a little tired.

"We just got in from Basswood Island," Dean Hillis, one of the guides, said. "We spent the night there."

They were from Camp Amnicon, located near the Brule River, and were sponsored by Central Lutheran Church in Minneapolis—twenty-six young people from different walks of life. Many were from congregation families, and some were from the church's outreach program for inner-city youths, which encompassed a few in drug rehabilitation programs. There were three leaders, including Dean, directing a journey through the islands that combined wilderness living with religious instruction. Some of the Voyageurs had never been in the wilderness or in a canoe before.

"We've got debutants who have to cope with other people for the first time," Dean said, "and we've got some inner-city kids who have to learn how to get along. But in a canoe, everyone realizes they're in the same boat—you have to cooperate to get anywhere. It's been a great learning experience."

I could imagine this polyglot group of greenhorns out for the first time. What a maddening challenge for any camp counselor, much less for one in a canoe. But Dean seemed nonplussed.

"How was the night on the island?" I asked.

"Not very restful," he said. "But I expect it was fairly authentic for our studies. The mosquitoes were out something awful. It must have been a difficult life for the original Voyageurs, too. Not only did they have to put up with mosquitoes, but with getting up at four o'clock in the morning and usually eating their supper at nine in the evening. The rest of the time, they paddled."

I was staring at the canoes, remembering where I had first seen vessels like these. These looked just like the birchbark canoes gliding along in the mists of the north shore, Voyageurs at their paddles, in the old painting in the Minnesota Historical Society Building.

Dean told me that the modern canoes are 35 feet long and carry from twelve to sixteen people—just like the ones originally used on Superior. But there the similarities end. "The newer ones weigh six hundred pounds each," he pointed out. "The original ones made of birchbark weighed only two-fifty to three hundred pounds."

That was an amazingly low weight, especially since the

birch canoes could carry 6 to 8 tons of goods. There was another difference between modern maintenance-free fiberglass models and the boats the first Voyageurs used.

"On a good day," Dean said, "they spent at least two hours patching their birchbark canoes. We try to get into the lake early, like the Voyageurs," he continued, "because Lake Superior has a nasty habit at about ten o'clock of picking up three fat waves and combining them into one big wave. It's not fun then, even in the new canoes."

It was time for them to leave, and in short order, they had their gear washed, their grill packed, and one by one got into the two canoes, which they had named *Gabriel* and *Shalom*.

"Why don't you join us?" Dean asked.

I thought a moment. "I'll run down to see you somewhere off Oak Island."

The large canoes were maneuvered by paddling on either side and by steering with a stern paddle, and they were awkward to handle in the confined waters of the marina. But once through the breakwater and in the channel they picked up speed, heading toward a northern island.

The canoes were an impressive sight as I caught up with them after hard sailing. Over the waters came the command of the bow man to the Voyageurs, "Salute!" I saw all paddles come out of the water, raised up straight in a row, red blades flashing in the light.

Suddenly I realized that they were wishing me well on my own voyage of discovery.

I watched the Voyageurs swing around the island and then I sailed back to Red Cliff. I wanted to visit an Ojibway center overlooking the waters beside Red Cliff. The Buffalo Art Center, erected by the Ojibway and open to the public, was a soaring wing of architecture that looked as if it had momentarily perched on land.

The center included many Native American historical

craft and art exhibits. I found one contemporary painting particularly arresting : It showed a Native American in traditional dress holding a 35-mm camera to his eye. I was struck by the oddity of what, except for the modern camera, could have been a centuries-old scene on Superior. But the man's face was hidden, and the camera's blackness upon the man's face was emphasized.

The painting was the work of a young Chippewa artist, Walter Bresette, whom many regarded as a leading tribal visionary and spokesman. Someone on Madeline Island had suggested I look him up.

The artist lived in reservation housing, a modern condominium high up on a hill overlooking Superior. He worked at home so he could tend to his daughter, Claudia, while his wife worked at the cultural center. He was a gregarious, powerfully built man in his mid-thirties, with a thick chest and hands that seemed delicate for his body.

"At first, I wanted to escape from the shores of the Red Cliff Indian Reservation," Walter said in a slow, clear voice, telling me some of the background to his painting. "Because I was in a white world, I wanted to find whatever I could that would help me fit in. I experimented as a young man with many different philosophies, and finally came to the conclusion that those of the Lake Superior Chippewa are as strong and as relevant as any."

"Did you have any crises before you came to that opinion ?" I asked.

"I went with this country through the Vietnam War, then all the crises in the sixties, and then some personal crises. I needed to center and stabilize. I remember when I first went to our traditional Feast for the Dead, we had to sit down and sing songs, and the medicine man kept motioning for me to join him on the drums. Finally, I went over, but I had to tell him that I didn't know the songs. He said, ' If you sit down long enough, you 'll learn them.' "

"Do you know them ? "

There was silence. "I guess I didn't sit down long enough yet." He looked at me. "Where are you headed?"

"Around Superior," I said, explaining that in part it was a voyage of personal discovery for me. "I just came from Madeline Island."

Walter's eyes seemed to look off into the distance. "We were supposed to end up somewhere to thrive as a people, and the Megis shell would shine over an island."

"And that island was . . . ?"

Walter nodded; I began to recall the legend. The Ojibway had left their home on the Gulf of St. Lawrence in about 1490 when the Megis, a great white shell that is a religious symbol, had beckoned them. All along their journey westward, it had appeared, then mysteriously disappeared, until finally it led the tribe to Madeline Island.

"When I go there now," Walter said, "I look over the graveyard and beyond to see the yacht club. I see the masts. But they look like crucifixes to me. . . ."

"Crucifixes . . . meaning what?"

"I don't see yachts, I don't see development: I see my people dead."

"On Madeline?"

"On Madeline! They're gone now—only three or four tribal members remain. But Madeline is one of the most important islands on North America. The Megis shell *was* there." He paused and then corrected himself. "I still think it might be there. Perhaps I haven't sat down long enough to see it or to hear it.

"But," he continued, "there are people who will someday share what they see. I guess I'd like to be one of those who share."

He told me that the Chippewa nation needed to assert itself more. "What we are talking about is the development of our community, refinement of our methods of government, and the exercise of our sovereign rights. We are talking about exhibiting one of the true fundamentals of democracy: the ability to be different. It's important that some of us become experts in the English language, in English thoughts, and in English acts of law. We've started . . . and found some real interesting things. Maybe someday we'll do a study on white America."

We walked outside, along the ridge overlooking Superior. "You come to Wisconsin and you see the lake," Walter was telling me, somewhat sadly. "The people who were here a hundred years ago saw a different world."

Here, the lakeshore was protected, but elsewhere, the forests had undergone tremendous ravaging. "The pine are our buffalo, and we know the impact the buffalo had on the Plains Indians. They took away the pine from us and they did such tremendous damage nobody even knows what it is. It devastates everyone who comes here because something is missing. They took away our forests, but they can't take away our lake."

He began to think of the future. "One of the reasons we set up the cultural center is to celebrate a number of things, and to share in that celebration. One of those is our unique proximity to Lake Superior as well as our culture. We've begun to design programs to bring people to Red Cliff, to let them find their strengths and work on their self-confidence, and to give them a whole new experience—a Lake Superior experience. It would be with small craft, doing some wilderness living on the islands, introducing them to sweat lodges, and letting them learn a different way of listening to sound and drums. Perhaps we can talk to them about some of the legends that were born here on the shores of Gitche Gumee."

I looked toward the lake. A fresh breeze was blowing through the pines.

6

THE OLD FISHING VILLAGE OF CORNUCOPIA

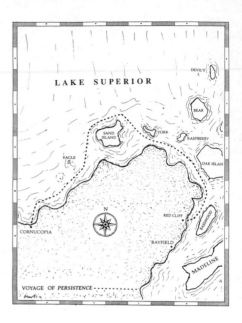

LAKE SUPERIOR

DEVIL'S I.

BEAR

SAND ISLAND

YORK

RASPBERRY

EAGLE

OAK ISLAN

N

RED CLIFF

BASSWOOD

CORNUCOPIA

BAYFIELD

MADELINE

VOYAGE OF *PERSISTENCE* - - - -

THE MORNING WAS MISTY GRAY AND THE WATERS WERE relatively quiet, just rolling with a few small waves. Weather 1, the continuous National Weather Service report I received on my VHF radio, had forecast a beautiful day on Superior, with southerly winds and light seas. I was leaving the protection of the islands, and for the first time venturing into Superior's open waters.

As I neared Oak Island, the tallest of the Apostles with an elevation of over 1,000 feet, I headed on a northwesterly course that would take me past Raspberry and then York islands, well off Point Detour. My destination was the colorful old fishing village of Cornucopia, Wisconsin.

I was about halfway to Sand Island, running under the power of my outboard, when a gusty wind suddenly arose. I glanced at my watch: nearly 10:00 A.M. Superior was right on time.

The wind increased and the fresh water began to march toward me in steadily growing waves; my bow began bobbing to meet them. Suddenly, *Persistence* sliced into the top of one, sheering off a little water, and then, with a *whump*, dived into the trough behind it, only to catch her bow tip in another wave. Water rushed back over the deck toward me.

I reduced my speed. *Persistence* needed a few more seconds to lift her bow over the oncoming waves. They were not especially high, perhaps 3 or 4 feet, but they were steep. I reminded myself I was in a small boat; I had to be patient.

Sand Island would be the last island before the open waters. Because it lies so far west in the 600-square-mile Apostle Island area, it is not often visited. But at one time, Sand Island had been a friendly place. There had been a village—begun by a Civil War veteran and settled by Norwegian fishermen and their families—with a grocery store, post office, and school. I knew these were gone now from the island.

Off to starboard, I could barely see another island that the Indians had named "the island of evil spirits," or, as it is known today, Devil's Island. They stayed away from this grim place, with its strange murmurings—so would I.

The wind had changed direction. I held my breath, then hoisted sails. *Persistence* caught the breeze, heeled a bit, then settled down to work her way to windward. We were now on the open waters, but traveling well.

I glanced at my watch: nearly 2:00 P.M. I had not eaten since breakfast. Though I was unable to leave the helm for long, I could fasten my tiller in place for a few moments and hope for the best. I went below, found a dried-up bag of fig-filled cookies, and brought it out to the cockpit. With a cup of black coffee, this would be my lunch.

I noticed that I didn't need to move the tiller. *Persistence* would come off one wave with a slight flutter to her sails, her bow swinging around a few degrees into the wind and her sails taking a powerful bite of air. We would drive forward with a great rush, spray splashing up on deck. When her drive slacked off, she seemed to relax just a moment. Then her sails would fill, and we'd rush forward all over again.

My little boat was steering herself. I did not think it was

possible, but I was in the cockpit, relaxing with a cup of coffee in one hand, a cookie in another, while *Persistence* did all the work.

I felt I could go on this way forever.

Rays of sun were slanting into my eyes; I knew the afternoon was closing and I was many miles from safe harbor. Worse, as I headed along the forested shoreline with its rugged cliffs, I was not really sure where I was. My boat, however, was sailing slower and slower; the shifty wind had swung to be nearly on my bow.

On this 50-mile stretch of shoreline are only two harbors: Cornucopia and Port Wing. I didn't want to be caught this far out as darkness fell. Finally, I started my engine and began power-sailing to keep my speed up.

Cornucopia was off Siskiwit Bay (in Ojibway, "place where the fish are caught"), but I knew nothing about the port except what I had read in two books I had on board: a cruising guide called *The Superior Way* and the *United States Coast Pilot: Great Lakes*. The harbor once had been a lumbering center and a fishing village, and it still retained much of its original charm.

As I slipped along a shoreline area of rocks, caves, and forest, I remembered the words of a young missionary's wife, Florantha Sproat. In 1842, she had also made this voyage with her husband in a bateau paddled by six Canadian Voyageurs and two Indians. Inspired by the coastline, she had written in her diary:

> . . . the scenery grew more and more grand and beautiful, the shore made for the most part of high precipitous rocks surmounted by evergreens covered with moss of every kind and color, and assuming strange shapes. We passed . . . an arched rock extending some ways into the lake, supported by pillars perfect and beautiful, bearing on its summit trees of every size and many kinds, evergreens entwining their roots in every

crevice, mosses growing of every color—the whole enchantingly sublime. We sailed our large bateau between the pillars and beneath the rock and forest above. After passing this we came to that which was still more grand—a large mass of rock with forest above supported by innumerable pillars, extending as far as the eye could reach, the water dashing among them, sounding like deep and heavy thunder—the whole certainly aweing. One of the boatmen, who knew not a letter, said, "It is certain the builder of this knew what he was about."

Time passed. I rounded another headland and tried my binoculars. There it was, a long, thin line of breakwater extending out into the wind-whipped bay, and on its end a light.

Cornucopia.

Soon I was moored beside several brushes on a grassy bank. A number of elderly boats of various types were also tied up, and a bilge pump clicked on and off. Nearby was a huge old barn, and flocks of gulls turned endlessly in the blue sky.

The gulls were everywhere; they seemed to keep their eyes on me as I trudged up the sandy road in search of the town. I found the village several blocks from the harbor, tucked into the side of a forested hill. The main street in Cornucopia was not too busy. In fact, there was no traffic. The center of town included a few elderly frame buildings and a general store. I counted two parked pickup trucks and one car.

Perspiration began to pour from me as I stood there alone, wondering what to do next. The tiny town seemed deserted.

A small oasis beckoned. Without looking either way, I walked across the street and entered the town's bar and grill. It had a horseshoe-shaped dark wood bar and a small crowd ringing it that seemed amiable enough. The room was buzzing with conversations that didn't stop as I entered, nor did anyone look up. A good sign. I hated bars where everyone inspected newcomers. I sidled over to a bar stool and sat down.

"A beer, please," I said, as the bartender came by.

"That's a quarter," he said, placing a tall glass on the counter.

When he gave me three quarters in change from my dollar bill, the reality of having discovered a 25-cent-a-glass beer hit home.

Several quarters later, I ordered a whitefish sandwich, the local specialty, with salad and French fries—all for $2.25. The freshly fried whitefish stuck out inches from the oversized bun. I nearly ordered another.

"Something for dessert?" the waitress asked.

"Yes, another beer."

By the time I left, the afternoon heat had passed. Gulls continued their endless games of flight or looked down from perches. Near the harbor, old wooden fishing boats were propped up on sand dunes, their paint flaking off and wood underneath bleaching a silvery white. A small community of buildings stood like sentinels along the harbor. Some were weathered waterfront shacks where commercial fishermen stored their nets; others, neat, tidy shops.

Inside a little store selling smoked fish and cheeses, called The Good Earth, I was greeted by Curtis Johnson, a tidy-looking man in his fifties, with short hair and alert, twinkly eyes, and a petite woman, his wife, Ruth. The Johnsons somehow seemed to be much more than waterfront shopkeepers.

I discovered that Curtis was the marina manager and the town's mayor.

"Mind if I ask how you decided to settle here?" I inquired.

"It's a long story," Ruth answered. She handed me a newspaper article about a minister from a large city, and his wife, a teacher, who had moved by Superior to mind a shop.

I looked up, surprised. "*Reverend* Johnson?"

He nodded with a wry smile and invited me back for some coffee and a chat.

We sat down at one of several outdoor tables on a small deck overlooking the waters, and Reverend Curtis Johnson poured some freshly brewed coffee. I learned that he was going to Madeline Island's church on Sunday to deliver a sermon. I asked how he kept up his work as shopkeeper and minister.

"I guess when I think of the ministry I think of a totality of life-style," he said. "So it really doesn't matter what one does but how one lives."

"But isn't it difficult to be a shopkeeper one day and a minister the next?" I liked the concept but wondered about the practice.

He smiled. "The Christian is supposed to be a servant, and you can be a servant grinding a cup of coffee."

He told me how they came to live here. "I spent a total of eighteen years working in the inner city. Ruth had taught in nearly all types of inner-city schools. We both got worn out and decided we wanted to make a change in our lives."

Why here? Cornucopia was once a thriving fishing village, with twenty-two fishing boats and three hundred people, but now it was down to two fishing vessels and a minuscule population.

"We found this community was caring, quaint, quiet, and laid back, whereas Bayfield is much more commercial," he explained. "Here in Cornucopia, if you make a lot of money, there's something wrong with you."

"You haven't made too much money?"

"We've managed to get by." He grinned.

I wondered if there was still an influx of younger people coming to the woods to try to find an alternative life-style.

"There is some disillusionment," he said. He looked out over the harbor for a moment. "To live a simple life is not easy. In fact, to live simply is a very difficult task because you are so dependent upon yourself."

Persistence was berthed with her bow nudging a grassy bank by the Siskiwit River. Wildflowers bloomed along the shore, nearly intertwining us. I was beginning to feel rustic. When I had arrived, I had asked the minister about accommodations.

"That's it," he said, smiling as he pointed to an open-pit toilet on a sandy hill.

"Showers?"

"Lake Superior showers." He grinned. "Everyone takes them, in one form or another."

I put on my swim trunks, grabbed a towel, and climbed over the sand dunes past the outhouse. Far away, on the big lake, a foreign ship seemed suspended on the horizon.

I took a deep breath and waded in. The water numbed my feet, then my ankles, and got as high as my goose-bumped thighs. I inhaled sharply at the torturous cold, bent and dribbled water all over me. Then I ran out, shivering, but better prepared to be in public.

The air had been cold moments before, but it now felt warm as I walked back across the sand to my boat.

I was just settling in, back at my berth, when I heard someone moving about nearby. A tall, silver-haired man was pushing his boat out from its berth. I threw back my hatch, surprising him.

"Didn't know anyone was on board," he apologized, and introduced himself as Mel Dahl, an engineer for forty-one years with Northwestern Bell in Minneapolis. He had retired to live five months out of the year at nearby Bark Point.

"How's fishing here?" I asked, looking at his sleek fiberglass fishing boat.

"Best on the shore. And I know, because I used to live near here."

My instincts were aroused; I asked where.

"I was born and raised on Sand Island, in East Bay, on July Fourth, 1911."

Now I knew. Here was one of the last of the survivors of that Norwegian fishing village on Sand Island I had sailed past.

He sensed my interest and soon he was talking about his life on the island. "My mother passed away on the island when I was four, and I can just see her coffin yet on the top of one of the boats going into Bayfield. Then, when I was thirteen, my father passed away on the lake."

"What happened to him?" I asked.

"I stayed with him during the winter, going to school. We baked our own bread because the person he used to have bake it somehow made it turn sour. He always called me 'Kiddo,' and one morning he said to me, 'Kiddo, why don't you and I bake bread,' and I said, 'Fine.' It was the eighteenth of April and he was going to set nets—his first outing on the lake that year. And so I said, 'Shall I go with you?' and he said, 'No, you better stay home and take care of the bread.'

"He went out on the lake, and then it began to blow something fierce from the northeast. I thought it would take part of the house off. There were ice fields on the lake, and they started to drift in toward the island.

"I walked out on the dock and I asked the other fishermen if they had seen him. One fellow says, 'Yah, I saw him, and I think he had motor trouble,' but he didn't stop to help him." Mel paused, and then said, "The last I saw of my father was April eighteen."

"What about his boat?"

"Never, nothing . . . not my father's body or his boat. He was out about three, maybe four or five miles straight into the lake from Sand Island. If he had motor trouble, then he got crushed in the ice field. When that stuff comes in, it has no mercy; it just takes you, and that's it.

"The only way we could get word off was through Little Sand Bay, so I and another fellow rowed across a couple of days after this all happened, and one of us had to sit in the front and break ice with an ore, and the other one rowed, because it froze as we went through. So then we got across and I finally was able to tell my married sister."

"Whatever happened to the village?"

"For a while, commercial fishing was good. But in 1956, almost overnight, the industry died. There once had been thirteen people, but they eventually moved off Sand Island. Then the government bought it, and they're not doing anything—they're just letting it go back to its natural state.

He shook his head at his memories of the island and his vanished family. Then he set to work on his boat and I turned away to mine.

That night, Superior began to howl. My boat was pitching about, being yanked forward and shoved against the pilings. I awakened in darkness, hearing a dreadful hammering sound on the transom.

"Wham!" I could feel it vibrate through the entire hull. I thought another boat had drifted over or that a huge log was pounding on the hull. I grabbed a flashlight and slid back the hatch.

The bushes were streaming in the wind. I crawled into the cockpit, and shined my light in the black night and wild waters all around my hull, but I saw nothing. I turned my flashlight toward the rudder. Superior was forcing its waters inside the channel, creating a current that slammed the rudder against the hull. I locked the tiller and rudder in place and examined them, but I couldn't see any damage.

Just a strange night on Superior, I decided, and I went back to bed. For a while, I listened to the storm outside, feeling the jostling of the boat, and then I drifted back to sleep.

The next day at about dawn, I was awakened by a tapping on my cabin roof, followed by, "Marlin, we'll shove off in a few minutes." It was the voice of Jim Frostman, captain of the *Ruby Ann,* and I rose quickly and dressed in the chill dawn.

The skies were still pink and blue as we headed out into the big lake. This was my first time on board one of Lake Superior's commercial fishing vessels and I was amazed at how cavernous the *Ruby Ann* actually was. She was of all-steel construction, 42 feet in length, displacing 16½ tons, and designed expressly for work in Superior's rugged waters. Beneath my feet was her black steel hull, but wrapped entirely over it and above me was a sheathing of steel. Unlike other boats, which have clearly defined deck, cabin, and cockpit, this Superior ship was all superstructure from the deck up—almost a boat on top of another boat.

It did not take me long to figure out why. As I neared an open door, I felt a blast of chill air. I quickly stepped back, imagining this fishing vessel in the fierce seas and howling winds of Superior's winter storms. It would be difficult enough to work on any boat in those conditions, much less on a deck open to the weather and the seas.

We were outbound from Cornucopia to fish mostly for whitefish south and east of Eagle Island. The motion of the steel vessel was quite different from what I felt on *Persistence. Ruby Ann's* hull worked through waves with the controlled motion of heavy displacement. She sat deep, shouldering aside light surface motion. Every time Superior moved, *Ruby Ann* didn't.

Captain Frostman, at the wheel, was outfitted in rubber boots, topped with yellow storm suit trousers and a bib, held up by suspenders. From his post on the bridge, he had a good view over the long deck and out upon the waters. I looked around, trying to find the other member of the crew, Jim Frostman's son, Eric, age sixteen. He was curled up on a bench, now asleep.

The day was turning bright and clear, and the waters were deep blue with just a bit of sea kicking up. I could see whitecaps, a sure sign of wind and heavier seas later on in the day.

"It has been terrible out here," Captain Frostman told me. "I've been in eighty-mile-per-hour winds and in waves where you go over one and down under the next. The *Steinbrenner* went down by Isle Royale in one of the biggest storms we had up here. It was a northeaster and the seas were humongous. They just couldn't find an easy way to ride out the storm. They tried running with it and they tried running into it; finally, the boat broke up, and down she went. Most of the crew got off her, but they had an awful time. I talked with one of the crew members later. He told me he had been sucked down when the boat sank, wondering if he was ever going to come back up. He had a life jacket on and he got lucky; he came up on the surface right alongside a lifeboat."

I knew that the giant steel oreboat, the *Steinbrenner,* had foundered in a gale on May 11, 1953, near Isle Royale's light. There had been a death toll of seventeen.

"What do you think happened to the *Edmund Fitzgerald?*" I asked. "The Coast Guard had reported the sinking probably was due to high seas and faulty hatch covers."

Captain Frostman shook his head. "When the *Fitzgerald* went down, the skippers talked a lot about it. They figured she hit a reef."

This was contrary to reports I had read. There had been no survivors of the *Fitzgerald,* so no one could say exactly what happened. Still, this was the first time I had heard about a reef.

"Have you ever felt insecure in the *Ruby Ann?*" I asked.

"No, not really."

"You have a lot of faith in this boat."

"Got to."

"Ever been on the reefs?" I looked at the waters churning over the rock-strewn shore.

He admitted he had. "If you get on the rocks, you've got one chance, and one chance only. When you go in, you've got to put her in reverse gear, and wait for the surge that fol-

lows. The surge and your own power might carry you back
out. But if you miss that, you're done."

We had arrived at his nets off Eagle Island; Jim left the
bridge and opened a large steel door on the port side. From
a separate steering station, he maneuvered the boat to the
first buoy, which banged against the metal hull, and began
reeling in the netting on a power-driven capstan.

He became very busy, adjusting the speed of the boat,
steering it, putting the net-hauling machinery to work, and
then pulling fish out of the net as it came on board. This was
not particularly easy, for the fish were still alive, wriggling
about. I admired his one-man show.

The net had caught several different kinds of fish, including trout and whitefish. Jim sorted the larger of these into
tubs filled with ice, and sent the rest aft on a conveyor belt. I
looked back and saw the young crew member awake and
working furiously. When they had the last of the net on
board, and all fish plucked from it and into the tubs, Jim
and his crew member went aft. Here the net had been piled
neatly, and I saw Eric douse it with something.

"What's that?" I asked.

"Soap," Frostman answered. "It helps the net go out."

Jim and his son began resetting the nets for another
catch. That, too, was tricky business. As the boat moved
ahead, the net pulled out of the boat; the crew's job was to
keep the net going out straight. This was a matter of twisting and turning the net, sometimes getting fingers cut by
the hard netting. The entire operation had taken about an
hour and a half for one net.

It seemed to me that fishing Superior was not only hard
work, but with all the whirling, clanking machinery, it also
took a considerable amount of physical agility. Today we
were fishing in relative calm; I wondered what it would be
like when the lake began to freshen up.

Captain Frostman went back to the helm, and as we
powered toward the next gill net, he began to eat the first of

several large sandwiches. I thought this was unusual for so early in the morning, but he and his crew had been working hard. I helped myself to my thermos of coffee and the bag of dried fruits and nuts I had brought on board. I turned to see that Eric was lying down again and appeared to be snoozing.

"Is Eric going to take over when you retire?" I asked.

"No way," Jim said. "He's going on to school."

"Any reason you don't want him to be a fisherman?"

"Yes. We've been curtailed and cut back so bad we just can't survive. I don't think we will. Fishing was a thriving industry up here at one time, but the lamprey moved in and then the smelt came. The smelt cleaned up the herring stock in the lake, and the lamprey cleaned up the trout and white-fish, and after a while, it wasn't feasible to fish. And then, to add to our troubles, there was the big Fish Sting."

I hadn't heard of it, so he explained: "Basically what happened is that the Department of Natural Resources in three states, along with federal agents, set up a false-front fish plant in Elgin, Illinois, and they solicited around the lake for fish. They said, 'We're looking for fish, primarily lake trout. We have orders for lake trout we have to fill, and we need all the trout we can get. They can be tagged or untagged fish.'"

I knew that untagged fish were illegal.

"This went on for quite a while and after a year, I shipped about four hundred pounds of trout to them. They were tagged when I brought them up there, but the guy said, 'We don't want them tagged, we want them untagged.' I shipped them two little batches of fish and then no more.

"Then in November, the wardens hit the house. Two of them knocked at the door, state wardens armed to the hilt. My wife was home, Eric was home, and the dog. She says, 'He's already gone on the lake.' They made a mad rush to the dock and it just happened to be blowing real hard that day so I didn't go out. They introduced themselves, and they were real nice about it . . . the ones I had anyway. I was given a citation and a fine around five thousand dollars, but several other fishermen got fined ten thousand dollars. And one man got hit real hard. Him and his wife and their boy, I don't know what the fines were, but they were terrific. They ended up going to federal prison for sixty days, and they had to sell their house and their property to pay the fines and the lawyers' fees."

Eric was working aft. He had been sleeping between jobs and I walked back to talk with him now that he was up. The boat was beginning to rock.

"I went out with my dad when I was seven," he said. "It was different—I liked it at first. But then came the years of getting seasick."

"A fisherman's son gets seasick?"

"Oh, yes, I've been getting sick since I was seven. I didn't this year, but in years past, I was sick every time we went out. Now and then a rotten fish would come up, and that would be it. All the fishermen's sons get sick once in a while. Dad used to sometimes, too."

"Anything help?"

"Taking Dramamine, but you sleep all the time. I take it at the house; then I sleep out here. The alternative is that you can eat all the time. Keeps your stomach calm."

"Want to be a fisherman someday?"

"It's dying out." He shrugged, somewhat apologetically. Then he returned to his work.

We were on our way back to Cornucopia harbor, iced boxes filled with whitefish and a few trout. I was amazed when I checked my watch; it was only 9:05 A.M. The *Ruby Ann* had tended her nets and now had about $100 worth of fish, that is, if the crew filleted the fish. Otherwise, if the catch went directly to the fish house, it was worth about $50. It seemed not enough for so much work, risk, and investment in the boat.

I was about to say something when Captain Frostman asked, "Have you ever had really fresh whitefish?"

"That's all I've been eating at the café."

"No, I mean *really* fresh whitefish."

"I guess not."

"Tonight you will."

Much later, when the sun began lowering over the little harbor, I put my frying pan on the stove in the galley of my boat. I tossed in a good-size cube of butter, and as it began to sizzle, added some slivered almonds to brown. In minutes, the delicate whitefish was a golden color and on my plate.

The next day I walked past the Cornucopia Post Office, which was not only Wisconsin's northernmost post office, but also its smallest, to a small frame building I had been told I couldn't miss.

My information was right. There are not many houses in Cornucopia, or anywhere else in the world, quite those shades of green and yellow. It was Roger O'Malley's real estate office.

Behind the counter, centered boldly on a wall, a bronze-colored plaque proclaimed:

ON THIS SITE IN 1857, NOTHING HAPPENED!

I blinked, rereading the message to be certain I'd understood it. It was here, the Reverend Curtis Johnson had told me, that the wily Irishman had founded the Cornucopia Yacht Club. O'Malley was tall and white-haired, slim as a walking stick from the Emerald Isle, and Irish enough to greet me expansively as a fellow yachtsman.

"How did you found the yacht club?" I asked, somewhat suspiciously. Cornucopia's small harbor seemed not quite right for such a grand title as "yacht club."

"By printing cards." O'Malley smiled ingenuously.

I took a step back. I had been to some fancy yacht clubs as a guest and I knew they were not only expensive but were difficult to join. O'Malley's approach was refreshingly different, but I began to suspect that among the kernels of truth was a touch of blarney.

"A few years back, my brother went cruising and some yacht clubs refused to let him berth his boat," O'Malley explained. "A few wouldn't even let him buy gas."

"Terrible. That was the inspiration?"

"Actually, my brother got in touch with me and I made up and printed the cards. Then when he was asked if he belonged to a yacht club, he flashed them our card."

"Did it work?"

"Absolutely. The sheer genius of the idea caught on and we now have three hundred members in thirty-six states." He seemed pleased with himself.

"And all over the world, people now honor the Cornucopia Yacht Club card?"

"Yep."

"But with three hundred members, aren't you *really* a legitimate club?"

"Oh, no!" O'Malley seemed to become alarmed. "The members would never approve."

I thought a moment. "Can I join?"

O'Malley straightened himself to his full height. "Depends on whether you meet our strict qualifications," he said gravely. "They consist of filling out our Membership Application and"—he paused dramatically—"whether you've got five bucks or not."

I grew cautious. "Let's see the application."

O'Malley carefully withdrew a white sheet and I looked it over. The first question was: My present boat is named . . . That seemed easy enough. But the next question caught my eye: If I *had* a boat, I'd name it . . .

"Seems straightforward enough to me," I chuckled, now filling out the form. I concentrated on the questionnaire.

"I do . . . do not . . . wish to take the required course to achieve the rank of Commodore."

I noted that I did not wish to take the required course and then came to the next item:

"I will abide by the rules and regulations of the C.Y.C. and will expect to receive notice of the Club's annual bash." I looked up, but O'Malley beat me to the question.

"Since all three hundred members from thirty-six states don't always show up, we manage to spend the five dollars per member application fee on food and drink for those who do."

I signed with a flourish. "My boat is the *Persistence*," I said, "and I am on Pier One."

O'Malley was not to be outdone. "Our Harbormaster and the Club itself are located on Pier Ninety-nine, so while you're down there, look for them."

I was puzzled. Cornucopia's harbor was small. Had I missed something?

"And if you ever find them, let us know, too. We're still looking for them ourselves." He permitted himself a small smile.

"Mind if I ask whether people actually use these cards?"

"All the time," O'Malley answered, his eyes twinkling. "All the time."

"Chicago . . . Detroit . . . New York?"

"Certainly," he said, proudly.

"Duluth?"

He stiffened a bit. "Well . . . that's a little too close to home."

I handed over my $5.

Walking down Cornucopia's main street, I admired my engraved gold, black, and white yacht club card, which looked very official. I was now a member. I noted with interest that I had card number 1044.

I frowned. How could I have card number 1044 when there were only three hundred members?

I smiled as I realized, of course, that this was just another touch of O'Malley.

7

THE SKIFF AT PORT WING

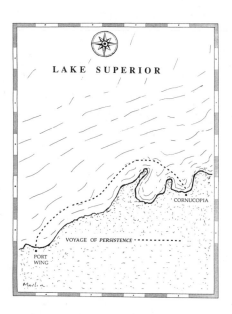

I WAS ON A SANDY SPIT OF LAND, PROTECTED BY DUNES and surrounded by woods. Ahead of me was a long, sandy area topped by a high dune; Superior rolled beyond. The quiet waters of a shallow harbor stretched behind the dock where I had tied *Persistence*. Reeds grew up through the water, and a mother duck and her ducklings paddled about. In the distance, heavily wooded hills marched down to the water's edge.

I had arrived in Port Wing. A large painted sign on the pier advised that if I wanted a ride to a saloon, they'd send a car. I noticed a pay telephone nearby with the bar's number prominently displayed. Another sign announced that overnight berthing was $5, and that I could deposit that amount in a small envelope (attached) and stick it in a pay box (also attached). I paid up, wondering how they'd know if I didn't.

Port Wing was the last harbor on my way down the southern shore of Superior to the westernmost part of the lake and the twin ports of Duluth and Superior. I planned to be here overnight, and it was time to see what accommodations were available. I found nothing near dockside, but was not surprised to find an outdoor pit toilet, but no paper, near the sand dunes. There was also no running water. I did not need it just to wash up, but for far more serious purposes—to make coffee in the morning.

I walked down a narrow, sandy road away from the dock, my plastic jug in hand, and finally saw someone stowing gear on a fishing boat. "Where's the town?" I asked.

"About a mile," he said, matter-of-factly.

Other towns along Superior's shores had built themselves up from their harbors. Port Wing was different; its town was divorced from its waterfront. Perhaps the reason was that Port Wing had been a rough Scandinavian lumbering town in the old days. In fact, I had been warned to watch myself in Port Wing because it got pretty rough.

"I just berthed at the transient dock," I said, apprehensively. "How can I get some water?" I held up my water jug for emphasis.

The man looked me over. "Down the road," he finally replied. Then the rough-looking waterman added, "If you need anything from town, I'll be happy to run you in."

"Thanks. Just a little water for morning coffee." I was surprised.

"Well, if you need anything else, let me know," he offered.

With full water jug in hand, I began my walk back. I decided my short stay at Port Wing would turn out fine.

I slowed my pace near the dock area. A wiry-looking man in blue jeans, broad shouldered and narrow hipped, stood very close to my boat, acting strange. His silver hair and beard told me he had some age, and as I got closer, I judged him to be in his sixties—obviously a person from the waterfront.

He would take a few steps, pause, bend closer to *Persistence* and seem to fall into a trance as he stared. I waited for a moment to see what else he was up to; but then he'd move a few paces more, turn his head as if looking for the right angle, and hold himself immobile, while he absorbed details.

I was delighted. I knew I had found a fellow boatbuilder.

"Nice job," he said, barely turning his head as I walked up. "And it took you a while, too."

"Seven years," I answered, wondering how he knew I was the builder—or, for that matter, that I had carefully walked up behind him, unannounced. "It's wood coated with epoxy."

"That's not how I build them," he said. "But it's nice."

"You remind me of someone I met on Madeline Island," I observed. It was an awkward comment. "He thinks the same way you do."

"Not Rufus Jefferson?"

"The same," I said, laughing at the coincidence. He told me his name was Bob Power, that he had lived on this waterfront on and off for much of his life, and that he was sixty-seven years old. Then he said he was a cousin of Jefferson. In their youth they had been everywhere on Superior— even rowing partway around the big lake.

"A fine way to travel," Bob said, "if you have the right boat. But it must be a rowboat."

"I've read some of the classic stories of the sea in which men have rowed across the ocean. That always seemed incredible to me."

Bob smiled. "Let me show you something."

I followed him to an old boat shed by the water. As we entered, I smelled the scent of wood, tinged with a faint mustiness. There were several boats hung by lines and suspended by pulleys from the low shed roof. I could tell from the patina of dust that they had not been disturbed in years. At the end, shining in varnish, was his special boat.

I looked closely at it; I could see it was built the old way, with fine, carefully selected woods, steamed and shaped into graceful curves that would welcome the waters. From the tip of its pointed bow to the wineglass shape of its transom, the boat's design had been refined over the years for one purpose : to be rowed.

"It's beautiful," I said, running my index finger along it. Standing quietly, I let its shape become etched in my memory. "I don't believe I've ever seen a boat quite like it before."

"It's a White Bear Rowing Skiff," Bob said modestly. "People, especially kids, always want to borrow it. But I keep it safe here."

"Looks like it was built just a few years ago."

"Nineteen fifty-seven," Bob said, pleased. "Actually, I built this boat from forms that I got from a man who got his from his dad, who had brought them over from Norway. There is still someone in Stillwater, Minnesota, building these boats from our forms, and he builds about two a year."

Bob explained that cedar planking had been used for lightness; I could see it had been carefully fitted. The steamed oak ribs were small and thin, but they were clearly strong. The stern looked difficult to build—its underwater lines joined together like a double-ended boat—but its transom swept loftily out of the water.

"Why the wineglass stern?" I asked.

"The following seas pass right on by and don't hit the back of the boat to knock it off course," Bob said. "You look at any old photographs of boats and you'll see they all had that same double-ended idea," he continued. "With the lift of the fantail, you can have following seas and get nothing over the transom, ever. The boat picks up on a wave and you'll just glide right down."

I do not know how long I stood, in a trancelike state, letting my eyes linger on the craftsmanship and detailing of this great old rowing boat.

"Want to take her out?"

"I don't know much about rowing," I answered, somewhat startled.

"You get onto it in a little while," he assured me, now undoing a cleat. "But the boat has been stored dry now for years, so the planks haven't swollen shut."

"How long will that take?" I asked, concerned about the boat's leaking.

He cocked his head to one side, wisely. "About twenty minutes. Maybe thirty. Then it'll stop."

A short while later, the White Bear Rowing Skiff bobbed gently in the water. I stepped on board and Bob handed me the long, light Sitka spruce oars.

As I rowed away from shore, water began to seep into the bilge. "Sure it'll stop in twenty minutes?" I called, still a little worried.

"That's about it, more or less," Bob reassured me with a friendly wave from shore, but I noted his answer was not all that precise. "Have a good time."

Alone in the harbor, I tried to get the feel of my first real rowing skiff. The boat felt light in the water; just a gentle pull on the oars would propel it. Then it would glide endlessly.

I tried putting my full weight into the oars: I shot ahead. That felt good, so I did it again. This time I missed getting one oar back in the water right, and was rewarded by a good splash of water in the face.

I was soon among the rushes, on the far side of the sleepy harbor. I rowed back in the direction of several ducks, which paddled leisurely out of my way. They did not take flight, or for that matter even seem alarmed. A little wooden rowboat just did not threaten them.

Time passed as I worked on my technique. I was seated low, near the water, which seemed to skim easily past me. The light exercise of relatively effortless rowing was exhilarating. Everything was in motion—the boat, the water, and I.

I looked down at the bilge. Water covered the ribs, but was not yet at the floorboards. It was seeping in, just as Bob had said, from the long-stored wooden planks. Nothing to worry about; they would swell up soon and the leaking would stop.

I was feeling adventurous. Sailors had rowed skiffs like

this across oceans. The little boat was handling beautifully in calm waters, but I wondered how it would behave in waves.

With strong pulls, I headed toward the breakwater.

The pier was long, and as I moved out to Superior, I tried to perfect my rowing. I had been using my arms and shoulders, not my torso. I tried to use as little muscle now as possible, inserting the oars into the water and then leaning back. It worked; we were now moving smartly forward, with less effort.

From the surge of water underneath the skiff, I knew I was nearing the end of the piers. I began to bob more as Superior's waves reached out to me, but the skiff put her bow into the onrushing waves, parting them cleanly, doing a graceful little dance.

A stroke from me and she'd glide ahead. I heard the water gurgle against her wooden hull, then join itself again gently at the wineglass stern.

The sun shone down hard on me. I was perspiring with the unaccustomed work of rowing, but happy—on the open waters, far from the entryway.

Suddenly, I felt a cold wetness. I looked down; the water now was over the floorboards, sloshing back and forth. When the boat bobbed a bit, the water formed into a small tidal wave that washed onto my deck shoes.

With a flailing of my oar on one side, I began what I hoped would be a quick return to the concrete piers. The waves seemed larger now.

I put my back into the oars; I skimmed. I was in a race between swamping and surviving. Water was over my deck shoes, and damned cold. I tried not to panic.

At last I came inside the protective canyon of the breakwaters and I saw picnickers sitting atop the ledges, waving at me in a friendly manner. One woman turned to a man. "Oh, look—a rower!" I could only manage a feeble smile; I did not pause or wave back.

Finally, I saw Bob sitting calmly on his dock, cross-legged. "She swell up yet?" he called over.

"I think so," I said as I came toward the dock, perspiring heavily, trying not to show any anxiety. "At least the bottom planks probably aren't taking on any more water."

"Told you so," he said triumphantly.

"Wonderful boat," I said, grinning now. "I went out through the breakwaters, nearly to the Point. I felt like I could keep on going for a long time."

"Then you had a good row," he said, pleased. He held the skiff as I got out, then sat down on the wooden pier, leaving the boat untethered. With his bare feet he tipped the little rowing boat on its side to let water swirl around the upper planks so that they, in turn, would swell up.

I sat with him for a while, talking about boats and the big lake. In the peaceful harbor, by the sand dunes, the world seemed especially fine.

8

AT THE HEAD OF THE LAKE

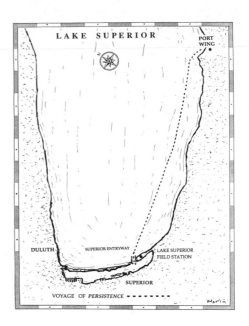

THE SUN WAS MAKING ME WARM AND COMFORTABLE AND the lake's gentle swells were lulling me to sleep. Repeatedly, I had to rouse myself. Coffee didn't seem to be working, nor did the cookies I had for lunch. The shoreline along the western coast of Wisconsin was kinder, more inviting: The rocks and crags of the northern part of the peninsula had given way to golden sand beaches. Ahead lay my port for tonight—the Duluth and Superior harbor.

As midafternoon approached, the head of the lake first appeared as a narrowing of the shoreline both from the south and the north; then the steep hills of Duluth came into view. From my cockpit I could make out the blue horizon of the Point—a long strip of land that safeguarded the harbor from Lake Superior—and on its northern end that unmistakable landmark, the harbor's huge aerial lift bridge.

I planned to stop at an old tugboat moored somewhere just inside the entryway to meet marine scientists who were doing research on the lake. Then I'd sail over to an island in the harbor, Barker's Island, and from these headquarters would visit Duluth—that picturesque hillside city where I had lived in the 1960s.

I could hardly wait. The cities of Duluth and Superior comprise one of the most fascinating areas in the world. Centuries ago, French explorers had ventured here in their birchbark canoes; I could imagine them on the lake sailing toward the Point, one of the largest freshwater sandbars in the world, not realizing that behind it lay a huge natural harbor. The Point probably looked as picturesque then as it did today, with sandy beaches sweeping up into huge, protective dunes. Now it guarded a busy inland harbor, the sixth largest in the United States.

The French had called the area Fond du Lac, which meant, oddly enough, "the bottom of the lake," not the "head of the lakes," as the English translation later read. Duluth was named after a Frenchman, Daniel Greysolon, Sieu du Lhut, known as Sieur Duluth, who came here in 1679 to negotiate a peace with the warring Sioux and Chippewa. After him came fur trappers, traders, missionaries— a vast fur trade for France.

But at some time, Duluth had begun an intense rivalry with the city of Superior.

Superiorites called Duluthians cliff dwellers. And the townspeople across the bay countered by calling the people of Superior swamp jumpers. The claims accent the differences between them: Superior is tucked away on gentle ground south of the great forests of the St. Louis River. Duluth sprawls directly above mighty Superior, ascending spectacularly upward on a steeply rising bluff; at night, its hills blaze with lights that can be seen for miles out on the inland sea.

From the beginning, the only entry for ships into the harbor had been near the town of Superior; this had brought shipping and transportation industry, and the related business that comes to a port city. By 1870, Duluth, envious of its rival's natural advantage and growth, hired a steam shovel to cut a channel from the lake to its end of the harbor. Angrily, Superior petitioned Washington for an injunction, claiming that Duluth's manmade entryway would ruin the natural harbor.

The government granted an injunction to halt the digging, and commissioned an army officer to hand deliver it. The Duluthians heard about the order on a Friday and knew they had just the weekend left to dig. Thousands of citizens carrying shovels and spades poured into the excavation to dig in shifts, day and night, until, early Monday, the channel was completed and Superior's waters rushed in to meet the harbor's waters. Hours later, the federal decree arrived—too late. Duluthians had their entryway.

This picturesque coastal area has had its share of Superior's disasters and has been buffeted by some of the lake's worst storms. I remembered the first time I encountered one above the canal. I was driving my car across the aerial lift bridge, a heavily girdered structure built to withstand the worst of Superior's winter gales. It was late in November; the bridge quivered with the force of the winds. Steering my car was nerve-racking; my tires seemed to squirm sideways in the gusts, threatening to propel me into the stormy waters below. I could only manage a few glances out to the piers extending a thousand feet into the big lake. Superior was piling her dark waters to the top of the lighthouse that guarded the entryway. The sight chilled me; I could not believe that anything manmade could ever venture out there.

I was wrong. One blustery, cold November night, I found myself in a bar not far from the water's edge, where I began learning about the wreck of the *Mataafa*. It had been on a night like this, a half-century earlier, that this steel boat had ventured out into the waters, ultimately to break up not far from the entryway to the harbor, in the shadow of the aerial lift bridge.

The ore carrier had been caught by one of the worst storms to hit Superior. It had been a northeaster, with gale force winds and mountainous seas. The *Mataafa* had ventured out from the canal, but hadn't gotten very far into the open lake when she turned and attempted to reenter. The *Mataafa* had actually made it into the entryway by about half her length, but, incredibly, outrushing water had pushed her back into the open waters. Her bow had gone down to the bottom of the canal. Her stern slewed off, striking the north pier of the harbor breakwater; her bow then spun out into the open lake. Beam to the onrushing water, a mountainous sea washed over her, with spray flying higher than her bridge. Her rudder smashed against the south pier and, out of control, she was carried into the rocks just off the shoreline.

I had listened as the full horror of the story unfolded: how people in waterfront hotels peered out over the thundering water as, not far away, men aboard the stranded *Mataafa* began to freeze to death in the night. Though thousands of Duluthians went down to the harbor to light bonfires and maintain a vigil, the men of the *Mataafa* were isolated. Rescue was impossible; no lifeboat could survive the wild waters.

As the long night deepened, an estimated 40,000 citizens gathered. The temperature dropped to 13 degrees below zero. People on shore saw three men fight their way from the aft cabin along the deck to the forward cabin. A fourth man attempted to cross the storm-lashed open deck three times, but each time he was nearly washed overboard. On his fourth try, he turned to see black water roar toward him. He bellowed a cry of "No!" and then retreated to the aft cabin.

At dawn, when the temperature was nearly 20 degrees below, the seas had calmed somewhat. Rescuers in a lifeboat rowed out to the stricken *Mataafa*. They found the men who had made it to the forward section huddled together, frostbitten but alive. But those who sought shelter in the aft cabin, and in the ventilators, lay so entombed in ice that their bodies had to be chopped out with axes. Incredibly, in full view of a city, these men could not be rescued from Superior's fury.

In that terrible storm of 1905, I learned later, twenty-nine other ships had gone down.

Now, as I neared the harbor, my mood brightened. I was returning to the area I had loved years ago, and the Point's sands looked invitingly golden. I recalled my time as a beachcomber when I had spent nights by fires built from driftwood, staring out into the big lake. Near the Superior entryway, campers were lolling on the beach in front of bright-colored nylon tents. There were even a few hardy swimmers where the sun had warmed shallower waters.

My first berth, I hoped, would be just inside the entryway at the Lake Superior Field Station. I had met the director of the research center, a young marine biologist by the name of Mary Balcer, when she and the staff had been aboard their old tugboat in Bayfield.

"Stop by if you make it into Superior harbor," she had said. Now I was about to take her up on her offer.

I had tried to raise the station on my VHF radio, and even called the marine telephone. No answer. I knew the station was located on the waterfront but had no idea where. I took a hard left as I emerged from the harbor breakwater and thought I recognized a large tugboat.

I picked up my binoculars. Something on the tug's bridge caught me eye—a sailor also peering through binoculars. We were staring at each other. He made large sweeping gestures, then called, "Come in closer."

I had been warned that there were parts of the Superior waterfront where one just didn't take a nice little sailboat. "I'm looking for the Lake Superior Field Station," I said, keeping my distance. "The director suggested I might get a berth for the night."

He grinned as I came alongside. "You've arrived. And welcome. Mary will be back in a couple of hours."

I was sitting in the director's plant-filled home, a two-story frame building that had been part of the former Coast Guard unit once located here. The field station was located on the end of the Point, beside the Superior entry. Across from me, with her long red hair and faded blue jeans, Mary Balcer looked more like a graduate student than the field station's director in charge of research and educational programs. Actually, she had risen through the ranks of researchers and had gutted many a fish while on scientific offshore vessels. She was now at work on her doctoral thesis.

Superior was the greatest of the Great Lakes, as well as the cleanest, deepest, and coldest. But some unsettling questions had arisen in my mind this summer that I hoped a marine biologist could answer.

"How bad are things on Superior?" I asked.

"Not bad—even pretty good," she said. "This is why there's limited funding up here. But it could go downhill. All you need are a few industries not doing what they should be doing or an increase in atmospheric fallout.

"Problems magnify," she warned. "You may have a low concentration of a chemical in the water, such as PCB, but when the little plants continuously absorb the chemical into their tissues, it can build up to be ten times the amount the water contains. A little animal will eat those plants and in turn absorb as much as a hundred times what there is in the water. The chemical accumulates in the tissue—it doesn't degrade and come out. A big fish will eat the little ones and have a thousand times the concentration. Each step up the food chain will magnify the pollutant. Though you have just a little bit of chemical in the water, you can end up with a thousand times that much in a fish.

"That's what happened in Lake Michigan with PCBs," she continued. "There's only a little bit in the water, but there's a thousand times as much in the fish, and they aren't safe to eat."

"The fisheries are in trouble, then?"

"They can't sell some Lake Michigan fish commercially because of the high concentrations. They can't catch those salmon and market them. Even the sport fishermen are warned against eating their catch more than one meal a month. And that just happened in recent years."

"And Lake Superior?"

"In some parts of Superior we are finding low concentrations of these toxic chemicals, but they are not widespread enough to close some of the fisheries."

"How about pollution problems?"

"There is concern about what has already been dumped into the lake. We've been doing studies on the harbor sediments and have found some heavy metals, such as mercury, zinc, and lead, in the sediments. They have been covered over through the years by the sediments, and so they are trapped underneath. But when you start dredging, you get them all back in the water. You don't know what has been dumped in that lake years ago. Some wastes were dumped in containers, but the containers corrode and the chemicals start working their way out below and may come up in your well water. Sure, Superior is the cleanest of the Great Lakes, but if we don't work at it, it won't be."

"What about the future of the commercial fishermen?" I asked, remembering my time aboard the *Ruby Ann*.

"This is what happened on Lake Michigan: They started stocking salmon and using it for the sport fishermen. The State of Michigan was very pleased, for it brought them revenue. They had people coming from all over, buying fishing licenses and tackle and increasing the state's tax base. The lake was being managed for the sport fishermen; the state wanted them there—they were bringing in all this money."

"And the lake fishermen?"

"At that time there were six hundred commercial fishermen on Lake Michigan," Mary continued. "Eventually there were fewer forage fish, since these were being eaten by the salmon, and the state started raising the license fees for the commercial fishermen. They put a quota on how many fish they could catch; they put a limit on how many commercial fishermen there could be. The commercial fishermen dropped in numbers from six hundred to less than one hundred."

"And the same thing is happening here?"

"We're afraid it is starting to happen here. There are few commercial fishermen on the lake because it's not economically feasible. They have a short season, they work very hard when they are out there, and they have a quota on how many trout and salmon they can take. There is talk of raising their license fee, too."

"They feel that they are a dying breed," I said.

"They feel not that they're dying out but that they're being wiped out," Mary said. "A lot of them would like to continue: it's very healthy, and it's hard work but rewarding. But they're more or less being outvoted."

The marine biologist shook her head. "A lot of people say that you don't need to sell fish when there is so much other food available. But someday you may need to harvest the fish of the lake just for food and protein. And at that time there may be no commercial fishermen left."

It was nearly midnight and I had the hatch of the *Persistence* open. I was enjoying myself. For Mary and the other researchers at the field station, the lake was a complex organism, the subject of a detailed, scientific study. From where I lay on my forward bunk, the lake was special, but it was a rather uncomplicated environment—I merely bobbed up and down upon its waters. I could sniff the swirls of fresh night air that had been scoured clean over miles of Superior. I could see the loading docks for the long boats; in one brightly illuminated berth, a huge thousand-footer was pumping out water ballast as it took on cargo. The ship was getting ready to begin its long journey somewhere.

We rocked a bit in the wind in the harbor, but the boat was tied securely to the dock. Directly ahead was the large tug, the *L.L. Smith,* and from my forward hatch, I saw that someone was in the ship's bridge. I decided to investigate.

As I padded toward the tug, I felt a definite breeze out of the southwest. By the rings around the harbor lights, I could see that there was just a touch of haze over the harbor. The bearded seaman I had met earlier was seated in the cabin, poring over a book. I stood for a moment, wondering whether I ought to disturb him.

"Permission to come on board?" I called. He looked up and seemed to glower at me. Then his expression softened.

"No need to be so formal," he said. "Go down below and grab a Coke from the fridge and join me." He was, like myself, enjoying the night air. As we talked, I learned that the sailor's name was Gilbert Stewart Porter and he was the captain of the research vessel.

Skip, as he was known on the waterfront, lived on board the tug and the bridge, where we now sat, was both his office and living room. He had been a biology student in the 1960s and spent some time in seagoing tankers for Standard Oil of California. During the next fourteen years, he had, in his words, "shipped for a while, schooled for a while," and finally earned his bachelor's degree in biology at the University of Minnesota at Duluth.

When Skip came to the *L.L. Smith* in 1982, he had immediately fallen in love with the 63-foot, 38-ton vessel. He found that it had been badly neglected and patiently began rebuilding the boat and her classic 5-cylinder Kahlenberg diesel. "At one point, the deck looked like a scrap yard," he joked.

The *Smith* appeared shipshape to me, a sturdy steel vessel that drew 7½ feet of water. But she wasn't bound to just harbor waters; I knew that the tug voyaged throughout Superior doing research and conducting educational programs for schoolchildren. I wondered about Superior's changeable moods and the risk of having children aboard in storms.

"We don't go out in bad weather," Skip said. "If there are whitecaps and small seas, the boat will be safe, rolling a bit, but the kids start feeling queasy—the teachers some-times, too."

We were interrupted by a sharp, long blast of a ship's horn. As I peered through the window, I saw the thousand-footer begin to move out of its berth, its huge propeller churning water. Slowly she emerged, under her own power, without the assistance of tugs.

"Won't the wind be a problem?" I asked. The boat had to back across this harbor and, it seemed to me, would nearly run into us to make its turn out the entryway. I worried that its stern would be pushed by the wind and swing over to us.

"Wind doesn't bother them," Skip said, not at all con-cerned. "They're so big nothing much bothers them."

"How about storms on Superior?"

"That's different," he said, growing thoughtful. "I've been out on ore carriers in storms, and even they feel the effect of Superior. In fact, they actually twist."

I was startled.

"You can look out over the deck and see the bow first going one way, then the other, in those storms. On thousand-footers, you sometimes can see as many as three bends in the boat."

"Doesn't something break, like the hatches?"

"Actually, it's amazing we haven't lost more vessels up here. But not because of hatch failure."

I frowned. "A report said the *Fitzgerald* went down be-cause storm waters were supposed to have forced open the forward hatches, filling the holds."

"Not from hatch failure," he emphasized. "When I worked on the ore boats, I put hatches down; they are mas-sively built and secured with clamps. There is no way they can come lose. The *Fitzgerald* went down for another reason."

He rummaged about for his charts, then showed me an area near Caribou Island. "Southeast and southwest banks," he said ominously. "That's where she may have bumped bottom."

"She hit a reef?"

"That's what I think, and some others up here also think."

Again the reef theory. It started to make sense to me. Still, this was different from official reports.

I looked up. The thousand-footer had completed its turn and was outward bound. It went by the tug's bow like a dark, moving wall of steel.

Skip gave a series of blasts on the *Smith*'s whistle— a salute to the ore boat. From somewhere forward in the thousand-footer came answering whistles.

We stood still, listening and watching, as she slid past us into the darkness. Perhaps we were both thinking the same thing: Just ten years ago, the *Fitzgerald* had loaded nearby and also had sailed through this entryway. I wonder what lay ahead for the long boat this dark, windy night on Superior.

9

TO BARKER'S ISLAND AND BACK

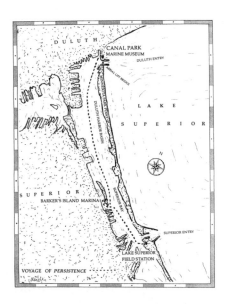

THE NEXT DAY, IT WAS TIME TO LEAVE MY SNUG LITTLE berth behind the tug and head to a small island in the middle of the harbor. As I neared Barker's Island, I saw one of the most gorgeous marinas I had encountered in my travels. Carefully manicured lawns swept down to water's edge; trees, shrubs, and flowers stood in landscaped glory; in the harbor, long wooden slips, carefully colored to match the rest of the architecture, held a luxurious assortment of large sail and power boats. Barker's Island seemed more like a country club than a marina.

Up from the shore were the carefully arranged buildings of a luxury hotel and a yacht club. A feeling of apprehension came over me. After roughing it for so long, I was not certain I was ready for reentry into civilization.

I had grown a little mangy during my retreat upon the lake. It seemed ages ago that I had left the domesticated, suburban life behind, along with such niceties as showers, haircuts, and clean clothing. I took stock of myself. I no longer wore a belt, nor did I wear socks—I simply stuck my bare feet into my scruffy deck shoes—and I got along just fine without underwear. In the mornings, I could dress by merely hopping into my trousers, pulling on a shirt, and slipping my feet into my shoes. Some people might call this unrefined, but not I.

When it seemed that I had worn my jeans or shirt long enough, I dipped them briskly in the lake, then hung them to dry over my boat's stainless steel lifelines. Showers could be found only in some ports; the lake itself was too cold to dip into. A little washup with a paper towel was about all I could manage some days. Though I remembered to shave now and then, such things were becoming less important to me. I figured that the winds of Superior made me clean, but I was glad no one was around to check.

I tied up my boat temporarily, walked into the marina office, and told the clerk I wanted a transient berth. I always hated that name. It made me feel like a watery hobo, but I guess that's what I had become.

"How long will you be with us?" the crisply dressed clerk asked. I thought I detected a slight flaring of her finely chiseled nostrils.

"A few days," I said. "Maybe more."

"Good," she said with an effort, assigning me a berth. She carefully pointed out that showers were in this building and went on to say that I was entitled to the facilities of the nearby luxurious hotel, which meant that I could also use its indoor pool, its sauna, and even its whirlpool.

I took the hint and quickly walked to the bathhouse. Hot water in abundance. I lathered, bathed, soaked, and gratefully spent time in the steaming water. I changed out of my much-worn jeans into a pair of khaki trousers and a fairly clean navy blue sports shirt. Then I slipped my boat shoes back on—without socks. I was ready to be a part of the life of this splendid little island.

Still, I had my worries. I was surrounded by luxury, but I needed to keep a certain amount of economy in my daily life. So far, I had lived on very little out-of-pocket money. Even here at luxurious Barker's Island marina, the fee for my slip was only $6 a day, but this was expensive in contrast to the $1.50 a day dock rental at Cornucopia or the $5 fee at Port Wing.

I looked longingly at the fancy restaurant's menu, but in the end I returned to my boat and my own galley. To eat even one meal out would mean to lose many days of cruising budget. Since I carried most of my provisions on board, I had the basics for meals anyway.

I was beginning to take pride in the quality of the cuisine produced in my tiny cabin. At first, I wasn't really certain how I was going to be able to cook—the space was so small. Then, too, there was also the problem of having only a one-burner stove. By trial and error, though, I had learned to plan ahead and be quick as well as agile.

Breakfast was a good example of cooking a simple meal on board. It required the combined skills of a contortionist and a short-order chef. The first step was to find my food and utensils. A loaf of bread came from under the galley area, as did the small Teflon-coated frying pan; two eggs from the bilge area, where they remained fresh next to the icy waters of the big lake. I found a can of Spam and a can of V–8 juice under one compartment. Then I had to get down on my hands and knees to haul out my gallon jug from under the forward V berth to get water for coffee.

At last ready to begin, I would sit down on the V-berth alongside the galley and lift the floor cover, which became my eating space. My feet dangled down into the bilge, which was a bit chilly.

Once behind my "table," I could not get up. The cooking had to proceed in a sequential manner. First, I made coffee and poured it into the thermos. I snatched off the coffeepot and replaced it with a metal grillwork over the open flame. On this camp toaster, bread would quickly brown in the propane's hot blue blast.

Bread toasted to satisfaction, I snatched off the toaster and positioned my small frying pan. Quickly, I laid up chunks of Spam, mixed in two or three eggs, and stirred the

lot together. While these cooked, I buttered my toast and
drank a small can of juice. When my omelet was ready—a
feast fit for an admiral—I just hauled the frying pan off
the flame and ate from it. This fine, hot breakfast left me
with only a few utensils to wash.

I took pride in my laborsaving efficiencies; I would often
remind myself that when I got back home, I would have to
show them to my wife.

Showered and shaved, I was ready to visit Duluth, the
largest city on Superior. It would be a homecoming and I
could hardly wait. As I sailed out of Barker's Island, heading past the salties and the lakers toward downtown Duluth,
I was reminded of the waterways of Venice. To be sure,
there were no gondolas or taxi boats here; nor were there
any of the wonderful little palazzos with their crumbling
brick, bridges, and stonework; nor, for that matter, gon-
doliers. But somehow the comparison persisted. What I had,
instead, were the wide-open spaces of a huge, natural harbor. I was approaching a city waterfront area, using a boat
for my transportation.

There was a crisp breeze but practically no waves. Normally, the two go together, but the thin peninsula that sepa-
rates Lake Superior from the bay is just tall enough to
prevent the wave action of Superior, though not high enough
to stop the wind. The result was nice sailing, without having
to pound through waves.

But as I glanced over my bow, I realized I had never met
a laker in a bay before, and now a thousand-footer was coming toward me. I had already been passed by several other
boats, and their wake had given me a problem. A powerboat
of any size could throw up waves to rock my lightweight
sailboat savagely. But a thousand-footer—a ship longer
than three football fields—what kind of commotion would
that cause?

The monstrosity passed so close I could see the welding

marks on the hull. Easing my sails, I angled toward the mountainous wake I feared, bracing myself in the cockpit. I was ready to get knocked about. Then she was past, plowing powerfully ahead, but I felt no jar. She left a wake of only calm seas. This huge laker, displacing tens of thousands of tons, glided so effortlessly and was so slippery in the water that it left barely a ripple. Hardly a twitch in the harbor marked its passing.

Amazed, I resumed breathing and went back on course. Soon I was nearing the Duluth aerial lift bridge and could see through the channel; no one was out in the open waters. But I knew that the salties and the lakers, as well as a few gutsy pleasure sailors, would be sailing out under this bridge.

I was reminded of my own first view of the Duluth rites of spring. When the ice is off the lake and there is a hint of warmth in the air, the sailboaters test their boats—and their own prowess—in an unusual way. As a friend explained: "You wait for a gusty spring day, then you put all sails up and head out through the breakwaters under the lift bridge. When you reach the open waters and the rig stays up, then you know you're ready to go cruising."

Near gale force winds had been blowing as three shiny keelboats came clawing out from the bay. With a clang of warning, the bridge began to open; the skippers charged into the long, wide canal that led out into Superior, full sails set. When the leading boat hit the open waters, a thunder of spray went over the bow, and the wind, now unsheathed from the shelter of the breakwater, slammed full force into the waiting sails. I winced as the first boat careened full on its side, waters reaching up for the open cockpit.

"Let her up!" I yelled. The boat's sails racketed in the wind as the boat itself levered around to windward, releasing the gale's grip. Finally, the boat fought its way upright, but the skipper turned the wheel again. As a gust howled toward shore, the boat capsized almost to beam ends; I saw the white-faced skipper hanging on to the wheel, his crew diving for the high rail. Incredibly, they had completed a full circle in the open waters. Finally victorious and satisfied the vessel had been fully tested, they headed back. The boat was ready to go cruising on Superior.

I envied the big keelboats. I had chartered these on Superior and I knew how confident a skipper could be with a "lead mine" on the keel. Once I was trapped unprotected in a howling storm off the Apostle Islands. When gale winds slammed into the sails, my big keelboat went over just so far, then stayed there. It had put its shoulder into the waves, then the tons of weight in its keel went to work and steadied the big sloop back. Though I had clutched desperately at the wheel, and my crew, including Loris, Bill, and our friends Mary and John Ketzler, had fearfully braced themselves in the cockpit, there had been no question that this boat was going to come back up. And so it did; I hadn't even touched the sails.

Persistence didn't have tons of lead weight down below— only a steel centerboard weighing 135 pounds. If she ever went over far enough from wind or wave pressure, or a combination of both, it was likely she would go all the way and not come up again. This worry repeatedly came to my mind. It was something I knew I would have to live with, and guard against.

Downtown Duluth was now stretched out before me: A northern metropolis, the furthest inland port in America, clinging to its hillside. The modern concrete waterfront was capped with a domelike auditorium. I wondered where to "park" my boat—it was *all* mooring space.

I eased *Persistence* around the harbor tour boat, past the tourists on the dock—some happily waving at me—and ducked into the first harbor inlet I saw. I seemed to be alone here; no other boats were around. Worried that I might get a parking ticket, I dropped sail and motored toward an area I could tie off in. As I came near, three picnickers on the grassy bank looked up, somewhat startled.

"Mind giving me a hand?" I asked, throwing them a line.

"What do we do with this?" one woman asked, holding the mooring line.

"Just wrap it around that metal thing," I said, pointing to a mooring bit. She bent down, wrapped the rope around it, and tied a knot with a bow.

I thanked them, and as they resumed their picnic, I closed up my boat and retied my mooring line. Then I ambled toward the downtown where I had once worked. Duluth is a very long city laid out on a shoreline between the hillside and the big lake but is not very wide. The downtown only goes up the steep hill a few streets. This would be a splendid walking tour; I would not miss having a car.

On Superior Street, I grew reminiscent. The first time I found myself here I had just gotten out of the U.S. Army. It was a blustery January day, the sidewalk was piled high with snow, a cold wind whipped down from the north. I had virtually no money and only meager prospects for employment. I had shivered as I walked, weighed down with two suitcases, until I came to the publisher's address and my first editorial job.

The office was located above a woodworking shop at the edge of downtown; it was dismal, dirty, and noisy. I had stood for long minutes at the doorway, thinking that all my education and work had come down to this: that if I was not at the end of the world, I could at least find it from here. Then I entered to begin my career in publishing, and my love affair with the lake.

Now, in the late July sunshine, I saw how much the street had changed. The publishing office was gone; in its place was a new and different building. I swung to the west, to an old and familiar haunt: the Hotel Duluth and its once-elegant Black Bear Lounge, so-named because an errant bear had crashed through a window one spring. The same bear, stuffed and mounted, had guarded one corner of the hotel's bar. But the hotel as I knew it was no more; its lobby was now a series of small shops.

I headed west, recognizing very little in the wake of urban renewal and upgrading. Even what was once a landmark watering hole for northwoodsmen, The Classy Lumberjack Bar, had been cut down, another victim of redevelopment.

Further west, downtown Duluth was stylish and gleaming, particularly with its new library fashioned to resemble a ship's bridge, and its Radisson Hotel with a tower-top restaurant that revolved to reveal views of the harbor and the hills. This was not my old, slightly scruffy city atop Superior.

Up the hill and on the next street was the Duluth newspaper. When I casually walked in and introduced myself, a young newsman jumped up.

"*You're* Marlin Bree?" he asked. "We've been hearing that the guy who's sailing Superior alone was in town—I've called all over for you!"

"Lucky coincidence," I said. He introduced himself as Robert Ashenmacher and began asking questions. Why was I sailing Superior? What had I found? I told him of the pleasures and challenges of solo sailing a small boat on the lake, of the people I had met on the waterfront—The Digger of Madeline Island, the Red Baron, Arnie the ice sledman, the teachers in the woods, the Red Cliff artist, the minister shopkeeper, the old boatbuilder, and the tugboat *L.L. Smith* and her red-headed boss and her skipper.

"There are some wonderful people here," I summed up, "but it really is a frontier that you don't get entry to unless you're a member of the water's fraternity. You've got to have a boat, really. Especially a wooden boat." I was delighted at the reporter's interest; I hoped he'd write something about what I found during my voyage.

It was late in the day as I walked back to the waterfront. I peered over the grassy abutment down to my boat—it was still there. But alongside my hatch, I saw a white card. I've gotten a parking ticket, I thought. Alarmed, I jumped down to the deck.

"Welcome to Duluth," the handwritten card read. "Glad you made it here." Someone who had seen me as I made my way down the south shore had written this thoughtful welcome and put it on board. I was touched.

Suddenly, my visit began to feel a lot more like a homecoming.

The next morning I was asleep in my boat when I heard footsteps clattering on the wooden pier. "Do you think he's in there?" someone asked, then I heard a knocking on my cabin top. I opened the hatch, blinked a few times, and met Wes Michaelson, TV news reporter, and a WDIO cameraman.

"We've come to do a story on you," he explained. "I hope we didn't get here too early."

"I talked to someone at the *Duluth News-Tribune and Herald* yesterday. . . ."

"It's all over the paper today," Wes said.

With that he got down to business and mapped out his broadcast needs. At Wes's suggestion, I went below. Near me on the pier, I heard him announce that a lone sailor who was making his way around the lake was now in Duluth. With that, I opened the hatch and emerged blinking in the daylight. I said something about sailing down the shore and how impressive the lake was.

I returned to my cabin, and both Wes and the cameraman squeezed in behind me. The cameraman adjusted his lights, and I demonstrated how I pulled up the bilge cover and placed it over my knees as a table. The newsmen returned to the dock, and I eased my boat out of the slip, sailing back and forth in the harbor. Wes stood at the end of the dock, in camera range, and finished his report by stating I'd soon be on my way up the north shore.

"When will it be aired?" I asked.

"With luck, tonight," Wes said as he and the cameraman trotted down the wooden pier.

That evening I dressed in my least wrinkled pair of trousers and a knit shirt to go up to the hotel on Barker's Island. I planned to try to see the news report on the bar's set.

The elegant bar was filled with cocktail-hour patrons. When I finally caught the busy bartender's attention, I ordered a glass of white wine and casually asked, "Mind if we watch Channel Ten?"

Minutes later, the WDIO-TV six o'clock news came on—and there was my boat! I sat transfixed, staring at the set. The television camera seemed to linger lovingly on the *Persistence*, then focused on Wes Michaelson as he told about a solo sailor in port, and followed with close-ups of me throwing open the hatch and talking about Superior. Next I was shown seated on my forward berth, pulling up a bilge cover and scrunching over my "desk" to type on my portable typewriter. At the end, Michaelson reported my plans to continue up the north shore. It was a nice piece of work—I was impressed and *Persistence* looked great.

I sat back on my bar seat, once again aware of the hubbub around me. If anybody had seen the TV report, they weren't showing it. "That's *my* boat," I finally announced, pleased as any new father.

The guy next to me looked up almost absentmindedly. "Yeah, nice," he said. Then he went back to his drink and his companion. So much for fame, I thought, walking back to my boat. I felt better back on the water, anyway.

"Is that you, Marlin?" Captain Gulder asked over the telephone, sounding pleased. "We thought you were the one in the newspaper."

"I wanted to call and . . ."

"We're living in the boathouse now, but you wouldn't recognize it. We've got it fixed up."

I sighed—even my favorite little boathouse was changed. "I'm at a pay phone in the marina and I thought I'd call to ask you out to my boat. It's been a long time since we've talked about the lake."

I was glad he accepted. I looked forward to seeing him again, after all these years. The call had jogged my memory about one unusual summer I had spent in the boathouse.

It was located about 10 miles from the city limits of Duluth, on a promontory jutting out from the north shore. The small boathouse had two levels: its bottom was at the water's edge to be used for boats; its top was where I lived. When I looked out the window, I felt as though I were on a ship, heading somewhere too, along with the freighters, ore boats, and foreign vessels that seemed to glide in front of me like so many toy ships. I could hear the *thump-thump* of their engines passing. Some nights the northern lights danced over my "bridge."

On storm-filled nights spray was thrown high against my window, but some mornings the big lake was so tranquil that it seemed like a piece of glass. An idea had struck me. On such a morning, the greatest swimming hole in the world was right at my doorstep. I knew that this northern lake was cold, but why shouldn't I try venturing into it with some protection, say, a *diver's* suit? It was not my intention to go below the surface of the water, merely to survive a little swim.

I took the financial plunge. After carefully unwrapping my newly purchased yellow scuba suit in the boathouse, I gazed at it in puzzlement. It was made out of rubber, in two pieces, not unlike great rubber girdles, and would cover me all over, from nose to toes. I would put on the bottoms, which included rubber feet much like those on a baby's pajamas, and then the top, which included rubber headgear. Only my face and hands would stick out. In the suit's center, the two parts joined—rolled up into a large, watertight band. I would be totally encased in rubber, not unlike—and the thought struck me!—a big yellow prophylactic.

Carefully, I began to dress for my bout with the big sea. I put on my wool army long johns and, in addition, a wool army sweater. The bottoms went on fairly well, but something went wrong as I tried to put on the top. I got my head in and had the girdlelike affair pulled over my arms and shoulders. But I found that the strong, rubbery mass would not unroll further. I was suspended, with my arms sticking out as though I were the victim of a holdup.

I waddled out the door and up the embankment to the nearest house—the Gulders'. One of their teenage daughters saw me and ran off crying, "Mom . . . Mom!" Moments later, an alarmed Mrs. Guido Gulder came to the door.

"I'm having a little problem," I tried to explain. She turned away momentarily; I could see her shoulders shake, barely suppressing her mirth. I bent over at the waist, supplicatingly, my arms extending in front. "If you could just help get it off . . . ."

Now I was certain I heard laughter, but then I felt strong hands grab the suit. They tugged one way, as I tried to help by tugging the other. I fell backward, but now the suit top was nearly off.

"Thanks," I said, emerging glassy-eyed. As I tottered away I distinctly heard gales of laughter, not at all muffled by the closed kitchen door.

It was days later before I worked up enough courage to try my diving suit again. This time, I took care to ensure I rolled the center up carefully so that it would unroll evenly, and not snag. Resplendently yellow all over, except for a red face and white hands, I walked down the precarious rocky slope to the water's edge. Superior was foaming that day from high winds, with a sizable chop running across its surface. I paused, wondering if I really ought to press my luck again.

Suddenly, I turned around to glance up at the hill. There was the Gulder family lined up on the bank, waiting to see what their obviously strange boathouse occupant was up to next.

Attempting to look nonchalant, I began walking into the water. I felt the cold pressing my feet and then my legs. Keep going! I told myself. As the waves pushed at me, I noticed I had buoyancy in the suit. I walked out until the waves were waist high, and, screwing up my courage, I sat down slowly in the water.

Immediately, my hands began to sting and my face hurt from the icy water. But, as I bobbed up and down, now nearly on my back, I noticed that the acute pain went away in about a minute and after that, the discomfort was tolerable. Besides, there were other distractions—for example, the waves, trying to push me down, up, and around. I hardly heard the sound of the wind.

I attempted a few quick swimming strokes, just to prove my mastery of the elements, then hurriedly clambered back on shore, to what I thought was a pattering of applause.

From these humble beginnings, I gained a passion for meeting Superior head-on that was to remain. Nearly every evening, I would hurry into my diving suit and head out into the big lake for a swim. Soon I added a diving mask, snorkel, and a pair of yellow flippers.

I loved the calm days when I could swim with my mask underwater, breathing through my snorkel, peering into Superior's depths, as an occasional fish swam by. But mostly I saw dark, jagged rocks, and when I went down to explore, I found pieces of wreckage and debris. Sometimes the lake was crystal and it made me feel like I was floating on air. But other times the lake was leaden and dark, and I could barely see my outstretched hand.

I felt quite safe in my diving suit. The air trapped in my wool army underwear, as well as in the rubber suit, made me so buoyant that I had to swim hard to churn my way under. I would float like cork on top of the water until I purchased a belt of lead weights so that I could sink. Eventually, I began to go out in stormy weather. I'd lie with my mask partly in the water to see waves rushing toward me, like walls of water that were going to topple over me. If I timed the waves right, I could also take a little surf ride down their fronts.

Captain Gulder, even without his captain's hat, still looked every inch the Great Lakes big boat skipper he once was. A tall man in his seventies, he wore his age gracefully. As he walked down the pier I remembered how we had met. I had been in the boathouse one evening when his ship was in the loading docks near Duluth; Captain Gulder needed to go down to his boat—would I drive?

In less than an hour, we were on board his ore freighter, the *James A. Farrell*. This was the first time I had been on an ore carrier and I was amazed at the fine woodwork and the carpets on the forward part of the ship. He went to his captain's quarters and, with an escort, I walked from one end of the giant ore carrier to the other, looking at the hatches and the aft compartments. Going below on each end of the vessel, I continued my exploration. A ship this size reminded me of a big factory, with all its pipes, gauges, and holds. Touring was also quite a hike.

Retired after forty-five years on the inland seas, Captain Gulder lived in my old boathouse. And here he was on *my* boat. I was pleased.

I introduced him to *Persistence* and we settled down for a talk. Captain Gulder spoke nostalgically of the old times, even though he had worked twelve-hour days and figured he earned 27½ cents an hour.

When he began sailing the Great Lakes in 1930, ships were up to 600 feet in length and carried about 11,000 to 12,000 tons, with a draft of about 20 feet. They had steadily grown bigger over the years, with thousand-footers now the standard, probably the maximum size—if they were any larger, they would not be able to go through the canals— and a capacity of nearly 63,000 tons and almost a 28-foot draft. The lakers in the old days, such as his *Farrell*, had proper quarters to carry passengers, always two and some-times as many as eight. Often the passengers were special customers of the shipping company who received free pas-sage. "It was a privilege," he explained, "and in those days, it was a way to escape summertime heat." The voyages usually lasted seven days from Duluth to Conneaut, Ohio.

The ships had changed over the years to become as economical as possible. Though bigger today, he said, they operate with fewer men and their voyage duration is shorter; it usually is five days now.

The old ships never really wore out. "A ship can keep going on," the old captain said. "Those reciprocating engines run forever, so long as you reline their cylinder walls and take care of their bearings and shafts." Captain Gulder seemed a little sad. "They were well built, but slow."

"What happened to the old ships?"

"We must have sent one hundred of them to the scrapyard. And in turn they ended up in foreign ports. I don't like it."

I was interested in whether a large old boat, such as the one he sailed for so many years, was particularly hard to monitor, without today's electronic equipment. The thought had crossed my mind that they might be so big that the crew would not know what was going on. Captain Gulder shook his head. "It doesn't take you long to know about a problem on a boat."

Including hitting a reef? That depended, he allowed. "In fair weather, if you were to touch bottom, you would know about it, and if damage occurred, the listing of the ship or the draft would soon tell the men in charge," he said. "Most times, when a ship touches bottom, you can feel the rumble, little or big, depending on the damage, if any." However, under certain circumstances, such as a storm, a captain might touch and not know about it. "You can do it very easily. In fact, you can tear out the bottom and not know about it," he said. But the consequences would be known quickly.

Captain Gulder owned that in his long career he himself had "rubbed on a few reefs." Once, while he was a mate, his ship had been running slowly in thick fog and strong current and had hit some boulders.

"What a ruckus that made," he said. "You knew you hit bottom."

That reminded me of the *Edmund Fitzgerald* mystery. One moment the *Fitzgerald* had been in radio contact; the next she was gone. It was as if the seas had suddenly swallowed up this 700-foot steel vessel. Had the crew known they were sinking? Captain Gulder had said that even though a longboat crew might not know the instant they had hit, they nevertheless would know if their boat was taking on water. Then why didn't the *Fitzgerald* radio her distress—or even slow to get aid from a laker not far behind?

Still too many unanswered questions remained, including the question of whether or not the *Fitzgerald* had hit a reef. The waterfront talk I had heard so far pinpointed what was referred to as the Six Fathom Shoal area near Caribou Island as the likely "touching" spot.

"It sticks out a long ways, and others have hit it," Captain Gulder confirmed. "Most shippers feel the *Fitzgerald* touched. He was southerly," which meant that the big laker had been too far south so that the reef was in his track. "There are lots of opinions, however; and only those that were on the *Fitz* knew."

Captain Gulder had nothing more to add. He returned to his reminiscences. "At first I was sorry to be off the lakes, but not now. In the old days, when they had large fleets, there was lots of competition, but everyone had to cooperate. Now everything is different—sort of cold and impersonal. You hardly have any human beings around, compared to the way it used to be."

And there was one other matter. "Today, ships even have air-conditioning," he seemed to sniff, disdainfully.

I heard footsteps and looked up at the dock. There, with something large in his arms, was Captain Gil Porter, Skip Porter's father, striding toward my boat. He was grinning.

Captain C. G. Porter, Master Mariner, Commander USCG (Ret), looked every inch the Superior sailor that he was—a barrel-chested man with strong arms and a reddish face. "Nice little boat," he announced, and it seemed he almost instinctively took charge. He noticed my compasses. I had them all over the place: a large bulkhead Gemini, a small compass fitted atop my hatch cover, and even a compass over my berth so I could look up to see if my boat's position was shifting when I was at anchor.

"The weather is changeable up here," he warned me. "And where you are going there are iron masses that will throw your compass off maybe ten degrees. If you haven't had your compasses swung, you could be off a considerable amount.

"Now's as good a time as any," he announced as he stepped on board. "Especially if you're going up the north shore." Turning to Captain Gulder, he asked, "Want to go out with us?" Captain Gulder nodded his agreement.

"How do we do this?" I asked, surprised.

"Head out and I'll tell you what direction I want you to go by your compass."

I motored into the bay. There was a fine, fresh breeze blowing.

"Give me north by your compass," Captain Porter commanded. He was now hunched over his mysterious box and I could see it held an expensive-looking gyro compass. He was beginning to adjust my main Aqua Meter Gemini bulkhead compass.

"Sing out your heading," he said after a moment. "I need to feel confidence."

"North . . . north . . . north . . ." I replied, hunching forward, trying to see over Captain Porter as he worked on my compass in the small cockpit. It was more difficult than I had imagined to hold an exact, straight course.

"I don't feel confidence," he said. I had stopped repeating my headings.

"North . . . north . . . north . . ." I began again, eyes glued to my bulkhead compass. *Persistence* bounded about, her bow being slapped with the waves just enough to make hold-

ing course within a few compass degrees difficult. It took a
lot of concentration.

"No one's watching the helm," I said, suddenly looking
up. We were in the midst of the harbor channel, with boats
of all sizes sailing around. I felt worried; my eyes had been
on the compass, not looking for danger.

"Don't worry about a thing, boy." Captain Porter
grinned, nodding with a smile to Captain Gulder. "You're
in good company," he said with emphasis. "In fact, the
best!"

I realized my little boat was being cared for by these
grand old men who had spent their lives on Superior.

"West . . . west . . . west . . ." I repeated, now concentrating
entirely on my task, my confidence surging.

I had been on my journey for what seemed like a small eternity. In the harbor, the stars shone above me in a clear
northern sky. But their beauty did little to ease my pangs—
I missed my family.

As I tried my radio link to Loris, the static blurred our
heartfelt dashes and dits. Finally, I threw open my hatch
and walked swiftly to the marina's pay phone.

"Can you come up?" I asked. "A few days here together—before I shove off for Canada?"

"We'll be there on the weekend," she said.

When Saturday morning finally dawned, I went searching along the bank beside the island. Carefully, I picked a
few wildflowers and placed them atop my cabin. My personal welcome to Loris.

Soon she and Bill were coming down the wooden walk-
way. We all greeted each other as if we had been separated
for years.

"She looks great," Loris said as we neared *Persistence*.
She picked up the flowers and gave me another hug.

Then we sailed. On this rare and special day, the wind
obliged us, gently bowling my little boat in splendid form to
this corner, then that corner, of the harbor. We sailed to the

waterfront of Duluth, past the salty anchored in the bay; we saw the lift bridge, and nearby, the Coast Guard station and its awaiting ships; I came so close to a moored thousand-footer I could nearly reach out and touch its huge hull.

"Don't get *too* close," Loris said.

"Want to see some gulls?" I asked my son.

He looked puzzled as I handed him several slices of bread. "Tear off a few pieces and throw them into the air. Watch what happens."

When he tossed the first crumbs, we heard a whirring in the air, and there they were. A few more pieces of bread, and then dozens of seagulls noisily congregated around our sailboat, beating their wings and diving for the bread.

"Look, Dad," Bill said excitedly. As he threw a piece of bread high, a gull swooped down, with precise timing, and caught it in midair. Then others came in, and Bill began throwing the chunks higher and higher, as the gulls wheeled, dived, and cawed. Loris sat back in the cockpit, enjoying the spectacle.

For the time, the waterfront was ours. A little sailboat can do that for you, I thought happily.

The weekend was over all too soon so far as I was concerned, but it was glorious. We said our farewells.

"Take care of your mom," I again urged Bill. He nodded, then gave me a hug.

"Stay in touch," Loris said in a low voice. "I'll listen for you on eighty meters." She turned to go, and then paused.

"Take care, Marlin. We miss you." If she suspected that I would have an ordeal ahead, she did not let that show.

"See you in Canada."

"See you in Canada, *skipper!*" she said. Then they were gone.

10

THE MYSTERY OF THE FITZGERALD

THE NEXT DAY I SAILED *PERSISTENCE* TO THE DULUTH waterfront. As I walked purposefully past the warehouse district, I felt the wind pick up and sensed a distinct sealike feeling in the air. I pulled my parka closer about me—I had left the protection of the harbor and was nearing the big lake. Today, Superior's long waves were rolling in, darkly funneled by the breakwaters; nearby, they crashed against a rock-strewn shore.

I was on my way to the Marine Museum. I thought it would be the ideal place to learn more about what happened to the *Edmund Fitzgerald*.

The museum seemed to be beached beside Superior like a landlocked ship, surrounded by relics that had been dredged up from its depths. In front, on the grass lawn, lay a windlass from an ancient windship; not far away were anchors, propellers, and even an old wooden Coast Guard lifeboat.

I walked quickly into the dark, modern building and was soon staring at the *Edmund Fitzgerald*, the museum's diorama of the long boat lying in her final resting place.

Based on underwater surveys and photographs, the carefully built replica in three sections sent a chill up my spine.

Her prim bow section stood nearly upright, as if ready to sail onward. But a closer look showed the titanic forces that had been at work: a strange wrinkling of steel plating and distortion of the pilot house. Her stern lay upside down, propeller and rudder sticking up, intact. In between, there was no *Fitzgerald* left—only a junkyard of twisted metal and hatch covers.

As I gazed at the ghostly details, I knew the lake that had claimed her was also preserving her remains well. A display of color photographs taken by submersible camera attested to that. The pilot house interested me the most: it was here that the life and death decisions had been made.

I thought back to ten years ago when I had stared uncomprehendingly at the television set. The *Edmund Fitzgerald* had been considered the lake's most unsinkable vessel. Later, when I read and reread the newspaper articles, I could not believe that she was gone—like a Lake Superior *Titanic*. In her death she had become Superior's most famous vessel.

Unlike the *Titanic*, the *Fitzgerald* had gone down in an era of high-tech radar, when boats were equipped with depth sounders and sophisticated radio and navigation devices.

I walked to windows overlooking the lake and began reflecting. It had been from this harbor that the *Edmund Fitzgerald* had sailed at 1:52 P.M., November 9, 1975. She had loaded 26,000 tons of taconite pellets not far from where *Persistence* was berthed, then begun her long voyage through the Superior entryway, bound for Detroit.

It had been an unseasonably warm, almost muggy afternoon. Captain Ernest Michael McSorley, a veteran with forty-four years of sailing experience on the Great Lakes, probably had no reason for concern about the weather. The immediate forecast was for south to southeast winds of 8 to

16 knots in the afternoon, becoming southeast to east, increasing to 20 to 23 knots—gusty, but still good sailing for this late in the shipping season.

I doubted that a little bad weather would frighten Captain McSorley—he had worked his way up the ranks, from deck boy at age eighteen to the captaincy of the big ship, and had seen the whole gamut of storms. Some said the *Fitz* was his only love. He considered her a "lucky" ship, and so did his crew.

The *Fitzgerald* had been special since the day she was launched in 1958 as the flagship of the Columbia fleet, an honor that rated her a salute when other company ships neared. She was the advanced product of Great Lakes boatbuilding, with steel plates measuring up to an inch in thickness—a tough boat built to take Superior's worst waves and storms. At 729 feet, she was the largest ship to be launched in the 1950s and was among the fastest ore boats. The *Fitz* achieved a single-trip record of 27,402 tons in 1969.

When the laker was well out to sea, an hour and a half later, the Weather Service announced the raising of gale warnings on the lake. The weather was worsening, with winds gusting from 34 to 38 knots. But Captain McSorley and the big *Fitz* had been through countless gales on Superior before—they were common at this time of the year.

Suddenly, a radio message crackled. It was the 767-foot *Arthur M. Anderson*, steaming out of Two Harbors, Minnesota. Had the *Fitzgerald* heard the latest weather warnings?

"Roger," Captain McSorley replied.

The *Anderson*'s skipper, Captain Jessie B. Cooper, also a veteran laker, said he would be taking the northern track for shelter "in case it really starts to blow."

"I've been thinking the same. I'm steering for Isle Royale," Captain McSorley announced.

The big laker was now set on its course up the north shore. The *Fitzgerald* and the *Anderson* would seek the limited shelter of the north side of the lake—where the waves

Wayne Nelson, above, *high over Superior in his plane,* Beauford T. *Rufus C. Jefferson,* right, *takes a break from boatbuilding.*

Modern-day voyageurs, above, *salute Marlin Bree on his journey.*
Walter Bresette, below, Chippewa artist, at Red Cliff Indian
reservation.

The Reverend Curtis Johnson and his wife, Ruth, above, of Cornucopia. Captain Jim Frostman, below right, and his boat, Ruby Ann, below left.

Stanley Sivertson, *captain of the* Wenonah, above, *on the stern of his vessel, and Ned Basher*, below, *proprietor of the Rossport Inn.*

"The Old Shipwright," *Albert Leon, aboard his boat,* Perseverance.

1/ GOING. A wave reaches over the North Pier along Duluth's Ship Canal.

2/ GOING. Now the wave begins to climb the North Pier lighthouse.

3/ AND GONE! The lighthouse itself disappears beneath the wave in this photo sequence shot during a fall Northeaster. The lighthouse stands about 50 feet above Superior.

would not have a chance to build over hundreds of miles of fresh water.

By 1:00 A.M., black water had begun to scour the deck of the big ship. The *Fitzgerald* had worked her way northward toward Isle Royale, but conditions were growing worse. The barometer had been dropping steadily since 7:00 P.M., and the winds had shifted; a storm cell was intensifying, roaring directly toward Superior. The gale had become a northeaster, whipping the waves high in its 60-mile-per-hour sweep. Already the laker was beginning to twist and to bend, but only with the normal flexibility expected in such conditions.

The *Fitzgerald* and the *Anderson* were not alone on the lake. Entering Superior to the east was the upbound *Avafors*, heading for the port of Duluth. The ship's pilot, Captain Cedric Woodard, was growing concerned. He remembers advising the Swedish captain who was beside him on the bridge: "We sure as hell have got no business out here."

A veteran sailor who had braved the North Atlantic, the captain could barely hold back his contempt. "Pilot," he said, "it's only the lakes."

Throughout that bleak morning, the longboats battled the northeaster, turning to run in an easterly direction along the Canadian side of Superior. By early afternoon the *Fitzgerald*, approximately 9 miles ahead of the *Anderson*, was about to cross between Caribou and Michipicoten islands.

Here lay Six Fathom Shoals, a series of underwater reefs extending 5 miles north of Caribou Island. Also known as the North Bank, it was an area well known to both lake captains; they had crossed within about 2 miles of the shoals many times—it was their normal route on the northern run.

Captains McSorley and Cooper exchanged information on the radio: "I'm goin, to haul to the west for a while,"

Captain Cooper said, changing course to get the seas behind him. Captain McSorley radioed in return that he was "rolling some," but he added, "I think I'll hold this course until I'm ready to turn for Caribou."

Snow had begun falling, reducing visibility, but the *Fitzgerald* was making good progress on her passage between Michipicoten and Caribou islands. The wind had now swung to the northwest, and the snow became heavy.

At 3:20 P.M., Captain Cooper peered into the *Anderson*'s radar console with Second Mate Roy T. Anderson. "Look at this," he said, nodding toward the small dot that registered on the radar screen. "It's the *Fitzgerald*. He's in close to that Six Fathom spot."

Second Mate Anderson clicked the selector knob to change the scope's range. "He sure looks like he's in the shoal area."

"He's in too close," Captain Cooper said, then added quickly, "He's closer than I'd want this ship to be."

The seas were building by the minute. The wind howled at nearly 80 miles an hour; waves crashed over the *Fitzgerald*'s stern, threatening to lift its propeller out of the water. Somewhere in the beating, Captain McSorley had lost his radar; the snowstorm was making it difficult for him to get his bearings.

As the storm grew worse, at about 3:35 P.M., Captain Cooper received a strange radio message from the *Fitzgerald*: "*Arthur M. Anderson*, this is the *Fitzgerald*. I have sustained some topside damage; I have some fence rail down, two vents lost or damaged, and I have taken a list. I am checking down. Will you stand by?" The voice had not identified itself, but the men of the longship recognized Captain McSorley.

"This is the *Anderson*," Cooper acknowledged. "Roger on that. Do you have your pumps going?"

"Both of them," McSorley snapped.

Captain Cooper was concerned. If both of the big boat's pumps were going, that meant the *Fitzgerald* had severe leakage. The vents could let in some water, but not enough to require two pumps, especially two of the *Fitzgerald*'s. The biggest pumps could each throw out 28 tons of water every minute.

As night fell, the *Avafors* was taking a terrible pounding. The wind was screaming, blowing half of the wave tops right off. The sea was not just big rollers, but practically straight walls of water. The waves were slamming the ship so hard that the people on board could barely stand on their feet.

In 8 hours, she had managed to travel only an estimated 12 miles into the head seas. For 2 hours, she had not gained a ship's length. Her radar had gone out after two especially big pounders.

When the pilot house door was ripped off, the Swedish mate turned to Captain Woodard and gasped, "We've got no business out here." But by that time, Captain Woodard knew it was too late; there was no turning back.

About 5:00 P.M., winds were gusting to 96 miles an hour, with some wave heights over 30 feet. Captain Woodard, on the *Avafors*, answered a mysterious radio call.

"Who in the hell am I talking to?" he finally snapped, not recognizing the voice nor all it was urgently saying. The strained voice answered, "The captain."

Captain Woodard apologized. "It didn't sound like you," he said finally to Captain McSorley.

At about 5:30 P.M., Captain McSorley made radio contact again. *"We are taking heavy seas over our decks. It's the worst sea I've ever been in."*

The night deepened. The *Anderson* kept radar track of the *Fitzgerald*, now desperately trying to make the shelter of

Whitefish Point. In the green glow of the set, the *Anderson*'s first mate could see the *Fitz*, and by 7:00 P.M., something else. Their radar was picking up Whitefish Point.

Captain Cooper called Captain McSorley to give him the good news. "We haven't got far to go; we will soon have it made," he said.

"Yes, we will," Captain McSorley wearily answered.

A snow squall descended. The *Anderson*'s watch could no longer see the *Fitzgerald*'s lights, but they still had it in their radar.

Another worried query from the *Anderson*: "How are you making out with your problems?"

"We are holding our own," McSorley replied. It would be his last radio transmission.

Minutes later, the *Anderson*'s radar was blotted out by wave heights taller than buildings. Superior was at her worst.

The *Fitzgerald* had sailed into a "white blob."

At about 7:25 P.M. the mate of the *Anderson* squinted into the eerily glowing radar set. The radar beams again swept the seas ahead of him. Something was terribly wrong.

The snow squalls had lifted momentarily to reveal another vessel, but an upbound one, the *Avafors*. Behind her plodded more vessels, also caught in the terrible storm.

In between was nothing.

Without even a final distress call, the 729-foot *Fitzgerald* had disappeared into the depths of Superior.

The official Coast Guard investigation had positively identified the wreck of the *Edmund Fitzgerald* in 530 feet of water about 17 miles from the entryway to Whitefish Bay, Michigan—she had been that close to safety. The Coast Guard had extensively examined and photographed her with underwater cameras; a Marine Board of Investigation had been held.

The Marine Casualty Report, "S. S. *Edmund Fitzgerald*; Sinking in Lake Superior on 10 November 1975 with Loss of

Life" (USCG 16732/64216), dated over two years later, was a 107-page document headed by the commandant's report, which stated : "The Commander concurred with the Marine Board that the most probable cause of the sinking was the loss of buoyancy resulting from massive flooding of the cargo hold. This flooding most likely took place through ineffective hatch closures. The vessel dove into a wall of water and never recovered, with the breaking up of the ship occurring as it plunged or as the ship struck the bottom."

It had been a laborious, exhaustive investigation, in which millions of dollars were spent. The board's conclusion that hatch closure failure had caused the disaster was widely reported. Yet no one I had met in my voyage subscribed to this theory.

Thom Holden of the Marine Museum resisted this explanation, too. "Most lake carriers don't buy it," he explained. "In a modern vessel you could not get enough water from topside to sink the boat."

Holden himself looked like he might have come off a longboat, with his heavyset build, handlebar mustache, and neatly parted hair. In actuality, he was a shipwreck specialist with degrees in mechanical engineering, journalism, and recreational resource management.

"So you think she hit a reef ?"

"It's very probable that Six Fathom Shoal, north of Caribou Island, damaged not only her outer but her inner hull as well," Holden said, "so that the working of the ship opened up to let water in. The consensus is that once she passed over the shoal area, the *Fitzgerald* was a slowly sinking ship. The pumps couldn't work fast enough to get the water out of the cargo hold. She began riding lower and lower in the water. Soon she had reached a point of zero freeboard, and the seas began boarding her readily."

"Captain McSorley reported that this was the worst storm he'd ever been in."

"It was some storm. But you have to imagine that the *Fitzgerald*'s front end by this time was so low in the water that the twenty- to twenty-five-foot-high seas seemed much higher."

"That solves the question of the abnormally high seas reported by the *Fitzgerald*." I could imagine huge waves all about the vessel, but especially those boarding the aft section, rolling up the long spar deck, and piling up to the pilot house. The boat must have looked like a submarine. "But what about the topside vent damage?"

"They're not really exhaust vents, but vents that go down into the ballast tanks to release, or equalize, pressure when the ballast is being filled or pumped out. The impact could have compressed the air inside the tanks enough to cause those vents to break."

"And the broken cable?"

"It would have taken a tremendous flexing of the vessel to get those wires to break. That fence wire is actually wire rope and maybe a half-inch in diameter, and it's not generally tight, taut but not tight," Holden concluded.

All of a sudden, it made sense. The *Fitz* probably had had its middle section slammed upward by the impact from some terrible force, popping its vents and wrenching even its topside steel cable in half. It had to have been a reef!

I paused for a moment to let the realization sink in. "Could they have felt the impact?"

"If the impact was large enough, they could have. But in the noise and confusion of the storm, with the seas hitting the vessel regularly, if she simply touched the reef and tore, chances are they wouldn't really have noticed."

"Why didn't they call the *Anderson*, or put out a distress signal?"

"I'm not sure they knew they were sinking; at least, the majority of the crew didn't know. It's possible that Captain McSorley did toward the very end, and simply opted to run as best he could toward Whitefish Point. If he'd been able to keep his ship afloat for about one more hour, he would have been in a sheltered area with several vessels nearby to render assistance."

"Most seamen felt it was unlikely that the hatches were torn loose," I said, getting to the conclusion of the Coast Guard's report. I knew that the *Fitzgerald*'s hatches were one-piece stiffened steel and each weighed 14,000 pounds, so massive that moving them required a deck-mounted crane. Moreover, each hatch was set 24 inches above the deck upon equally massive steel hatch coamings, and sealed with a compression gasket. Each was secured by no fewer than 68 tension clamps, one every two feet. In the worst of storms, the *Fitz* had never arrived in port with even a damp cargo.

"The hatches certainly didn't lift off," Thom agreed, "and I don't feel that they could have leaked enough water between the hatch cover and the hatch coaming to have caused the vessel to ride so low in the water."

Holden paused a moment. "However, the report that makes the most sense to me is the one written by Philip Allison Hogue, a member of the National Transportation Safety Board. In his dissenting opinion to the board's findings, Hogue took into account that the hatch covers were designed to withstand the weight of only four feet of static water sitting upon them. He felt that the *Fitzgerald* reached a point of being near zero freeboard—just barely afloat—when the waves would have been boarding the ship regularly. Since the waves were boarding from the stern quarter, water was actually piling up, standing on the deck behind the pilot house. Under these conditions, it's likely that one or two of those hatch covers actually caved in, leaving a large opening in the deck for every subsequent wave to enter. Tons of water then poured into the cargo hold.

"But you see the opinion carefully didn't say what it was that caused the ship to reach that point. And that's where we get back to other opinions that the Six Fathom Shoal area was the cause of the *Fitzgerald*'s getting water into her cargo hold in the first place."

"Now the big question—how could she hit the shoals?"

"She was definitely in that vicinity, and there is nothing else to hit. Six Fathom Shoals charts indicated thirty-six feet above them and lakers can pass over them normally, since they usually draw about twenty-seven and a half feet."

"So there was still some area between the bottom of the ship and the reported depth of the reef."

"In a storm, you have great waves. The *Fitzgerald* could have been rolling or bouncing around, in the trough of a wave, and this could have added ten feet of depth.

"The end must have come suddenly—there was no radio call for help. Could she have broken up on the surface, as some claim?"

"No," Thom said, "because if she did, her bow and her stern would not be together. One ship we know did break up on the surface and her bow and stern are now miles apart.

I looked at the diorama of the ship in three pieces.

"You have to remember how she went down," he continued. "Her bow was heavy, so she was probably bending in the middle. Her prop was twisting her stern. Her cargo rushed forward. Together, these forces destroyed the middle section of the ship on the way to the bottom.

"She probably began breaking up on the way down—there is some evidence of this in the way her plates are torn. They don't show impact, but more of a ripping. There is no photographic evidence of impact on the bottom, but her stern is dented. Fact is, it looks like the bow ran into it on the way down. The bow does not show a tearing of plates, just some buckling."

He paused for a moment of reflection, a lover of ships. "You know, it's amazing when you see this inch-thick steel torn like paper."

Back at the *Persistence* that night, I felt restless; I had so many answers, yet something was still missing. By the light of my single cabin bulb, I studied reports, wondering if there wasn't something that had not yet come out. The extensive underwater survey of the wreckage could not confirm that there was a hole in the big laker's bottom, since the forward section lay on her bottom, and the center 200 feet of the ship lay in shreds. There was no firm proof that the *Fitzgerald* had struck a reef—only circumstantial evidence.

Weary, I looked out my portlight at the marina's dark waters and began thinking about my own diving experiences on the north shore; certainly I had scratched around enough reefs to know they all had stories to tell. Perhaps it was the reef itself that held the missing clues. I reached over to pull out the twenty-eight Lake Superior charts I had on board and soon found Canadian 2310—that of the Caribou Island to Michipicoten Island area. And there they lay, the reefs I had heard so much about. I ran my finger over those that extended out past Caribou Island; to my surprise, I saw not one reef, but a *series* of reefs running throughout the area, some as little as 5¼ fathoms deep, and covering a wider area than I had expected.

Both the *Anderson* and the *Fitzgerald* had passed within several miles of this unmarked bank. Survey work for the chart had been completed by the Canadian Hydrographic Service in 1916 and 1919—so long ago, and in such an unsophisticated hydrographic surveying era that I wondered how accurate it was. There was a note that said the chart was "corrected through notices to mariners," but these notices were of little help to me here, in my cabin, as I looked at the chart. I wondered how much they had meant to the *Fitzgerald* in that storm.

Curious, I began searching through some papers I had brought on board, and I found that in 1977 the Lake Carriers Association had issued a rebuttal of the Coast Guard findings on the *Fitzgerald*. The Association mentioned a *new* hydrographic survey of the Caribou Island shoal waters area by the Canadian Hydrographic Service, which had been done at the request of the Coast Guard Marine Board shortly after the *Fitzgerald* sinking. This had identified another shoal less than 36 feet deep. It lay about 1 mile farther east than any in the Six Fathom Shoal cluster that was depicted on either Canadian or U.S. navigation charts. The newly verified shoal, the Association pointed out ominously and specifically, "was in the track of the *Fitzgerald*. . . ." The thought flashed in my mind : They suspected!

All the information that had been uncovered prior to this survey, which had been made public, had been either from board hearings or investigation of the wreck. The approach that should have been taken, I began to feel, was to have inspected the new reef for evidence of a grounding.

From my own experience, I knew that a scuba-equipped diver could have gone down the spring following the disaster, when the waters were clear and placid, and made a thorough search with relatively few problems. If I had been on the lake at the time, and had a depth finder, I probably could have sailed *Persistence* along the shoal area north of Caribou, using the bottom as my "map," and run a search pattern until I found the suspect reef. That would have taken time, of course, but then it would have been easy for a diver to slip over the side to check the area ; 36 feet is not deep.

If a huge ore carrier the size of the *Fitzgerald* had rammed through the area, the rocks would have shown it. In fact, there would have been an enormous collision. The rocks would either have broken away, in which case their bright breaks would have shown clearly in the waters, or, if the hull did not break the rock, but flexed and bent before it ruptured inward, its bottom paint would have smeared all over the rock. A lot of it.

It was also likely that there would be other bits of the *Fitzgerald* on the new reef, such as metal scoured or torn from the hull, possibly even a section of a plate, her cargo, or some other part of the big laker.

The reef alone would be the final answer to the mystery of the *Fitzgerald*. If she had bottomed in the Six Fathom area, she would have left more than just a calling card to indicate her passage.

And now ? It was more than a decade since the *Fitzgerald*

went down. Superior, with its violent storms and quick waters, has a way of reverting to the wild. Any broken or scratched rock would no longer be bright or possibly even recognizable. Any paint on a rock could be covered with lake organisms, growth, or otherwise hidden or worn away. Any metal left on or near the reef might have swirled away into Superior. Today, it would be difficult to find traces of the *Fitzgerald*'s tragedy at the shoals; in fact, it might be too late.

But something else—important to me—came into focus.

Captain McSorley had not suddenly become careless after forty-four years on the lake and run his beloved *Fitzgerald* upon Six Fathom Shoals. He had avoided the reefs carefully, even giving them nearly a mile's free berth.

Then, most likely, thinking he had clear water ahead since no dangerous shoals were known or indicated, he had swung in a southeasterly direction. He probably had it in mind to get behind the lee of Caribou Island and give his laboring boat calmer waters in the terrible storm. Instead, he found a new reef.

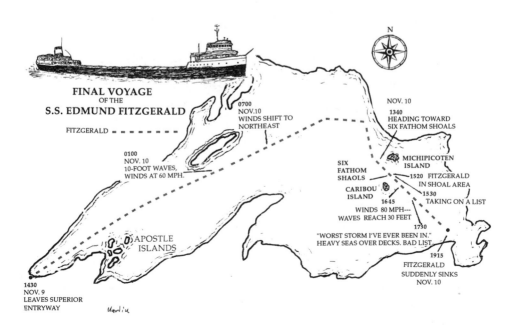

FINAL VOYAGE
OF THE
S.S. EDMUND FITZGERALD

FITZGERALD ▪ ▪▪ ▪ ▪▪ ▪ ▪▪ ▪

N

0700
NOV.10
WINDS SHIFT TO
NORTHEAST

NOV. 10

1340
HEADING TOWARD
SIX FATHOM SHOALS

0100
NOV. 10
10-FOOT WAVES,
WINDS AT 60 MPH

SIX
FATHOM
SHOALS

MICHIPICOTEN
ISLAND

1520 FITZGERALD
IN SHOAL AREA

CARIBOU
ISLAND

1530
TAKING ON A LIST

1645

WINDS 80 MPH---
WAVES REACH 30 FEET

1730
"WORST STORM I'VE EVER BEEN IN."
HEAVY SEAS OVER DECKS. BAD LIST

APOSTLE
ISLANDS

1915
FITZGERALD
SUDDENLY SINKS
NOV. 10

1430
NOV. 9
LEAVES SUPERIOR
ENTRYWAY

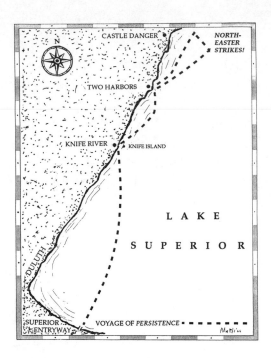

11

UP THE
DARK
SHORE

"BEWARE THE NORTHEASTER." THE WORDS OF THE OLD Commodore from Madeline Island were burned in my mind. He had been trapped by one on the north shore in his large sloop. "It was fierce," he told me, "not to be repeated. Just don't get caught."

I knew I needed the right conditions to voyage up the north shore to Canada. But as I figured it, a lot was simply a matter of timing.

The weather was bright and clear this morning, with a hint of coolness in the air. As I stood upon the deck, I felt a pleasant zephyr out of the southwest—just right to bowl me up the shore. On a day such as this, I felt that God was in his heaven and all was right with the world, and, in particular, with Superior. The zephyr was an omen. I made my decision : time to shove off.

I knew a little of what lay ahead. In 1870, the *Chicago Tribune* had poetically described the north shore :

> . . . an unending range of hills and mountains, indented here and there with beetling crags and frowning preci-
> pices on their summits. . . . Here are caverns which

might shelter the Titans, gorges which seem fathomless. Nature here is not in her pretty moods; she frowns at you from stupendous crags. Her music is the thunder. Her play is in the everlasting wash of the waves against solid granite walls.

My charts told me that this would be the longest and most inhospitable leg of the voyage. The *Coast Pilot* was more to the point: "bold and rocky."

Today, I'd sail to Grand Marais, 106 miles up the coast. It would be a long, hard run. If all went well, I could make it by nightfall, or maybe a little after. I hurriedly began my final preparations, then walked to the marina office to pay my berthing bill.

Suddenly, I heard a howling outside.

"What's that?" I rushed to a window. In the slips, heavy keelboats danced, clanging halyards as their masts whipped from side to side. My heart sank. Another omen, this one reminding me never to take Superior for granted.

"You still going?" the worried attendant asked.

I looked closer at the harbor. Cat's paws whipped across the water; telltales on yachts swung steadily. But the wind was still out of the south and west—a favorable direction. It would just sweep me right up the shore.

I shrugged. "Why not?"

Under reefed sails, I soared across the harbor and shot out onto the big lake. The ride was exhilarating, but I could see the effect these strong winds were having—waves were quickly being heaped into wave trains that roared at my speeding boat. One would slice toward me, lift my boat's stern up and sideways, and give us a playful toss. The farther I sailed into the big lake, the higher the waves rose. It's only wind and water, I rationalized.

But it didn't take much bouncing to help me make another decision: today I'd not go to Grand Marais, only to Knife River, just 25 miles away. I swallowed hard; it would be my last marina until I got a lot farther up the shore.

Hours later, I hesitantly approached the rocky shore, searching for landmarks. The marina was hidden, but I knew its entryway was located opposite Knife Island.

As I neared, I located the island, then saw a patch of white between it and the steep, rocky shore. At first I thought it was another sailboat, but it didn't move. I pulled out my binoculars and discovered the white was not sails but spray flung up from reefs directly ahead of me. I'd have to come in close to the headland to enter the marina. In this weather, I'd have to navigate carefully.

"*Persistence*, calling the *Persistence*."

I jumped forward. "This is the *Persistence*," I yelled in acknowledgment.

"*Tiger* here," came the unhurried reply; I relaxed for a moment. I had met him at the Barker's Island marina—he said he'd meet me on the way up the north shore. I was delighted to have company.

"*Persistence*, what's your location?"

"Nearing Knife River Harbor. The entryway should be just ahead."

"Good show, *Persistence*," *Tiger* purred. "Just checking my radio. You're coming in loud and clear."

That struck me as odd.

"Hey, wait a minute—when are you leaving?"

"I'm not," he said quickly. "Things don't look too good right now. Out!"

"*Persistence* out, too." I felt alone and puzzled.

Once I neared the rocky cliff, opposite the spray-splashed reefs, I could see the breakwater—my entry to the marina. Without a chart and a cruising guide, I would never have guessed that a small harbor had been carved into the rugged hills.

Then Granite Point overshadowed us. It was as if I had entered another world, quiet and orderly. I emerged from the rocky channel and smelled the fragrance of pines and earth. The sea smell of Superior had been left behind.

In the late-afternoon sun, the small marina stretched upward on the hillside, encircled by a dense forest. Its lagoon seemed incredibly blue and transparent; I felt like an intruder in this north woods domain.

The marina was deserted, but as sunset arrived, men and women began to appear on the heavily wooded banks, coming down to their boats. It was as if a little town had sprung into life. Just like in the movie *Brigadoon*. Some people busied themselves with the innumerable chores boat owners have; others cooked supper, but most just sat in their cockpits, mildly rocking, enjoying the quiet of the north woods evening.

A forest ranger stopped by to admire my boat. Finally, he asked, "Going to visit Two Harbors?"

"I wasn't planning to," I said. "I need to move right along up the north shore. Why?"

"The town is having a festival. One hundred years of shipping iron ore. You ought to stop by—maybe see our coal-burning tugboat, the *Edna G.*"

"I'll think about it, thanks," I said. I had heard about this historic boat and thought it might be worth a visit. She was a part of the big days of iron mining.

That night the sultry air turned misty and I heard rain on my coach roof. It was pleasant for sleeping. I didn't realize at the time it would be the last good rest I'd have for many nights to come.

My plan was to sail out of Knife River, stop briefly at Two Harbors, and then proceed on to Grand Marais, Grand Portage, and into Canada. Though I still had a favorable wind, I didn't want to get stuck somewhere, hit a storm, or run out of fuel.

I planned to gas up for my push up the shore, but the marina attendant wasn't around. By the time I got my tank full and shoved off, it was late morning. I didn't hurry, though; I figured I could still be in Two Harbors by around noon—in time for the festival and, I hoped, a hearty lunch.

I looked forward to a break from my usual fare of canned foods and cookies.

The shoreline became increasingly craggy, and, rounding one headland, I came to large breakwaters and a lighthouse. Ahead lay tall iron ore loading docks, dark and rusty red; seagulls soared over the nearly still waters. Up the hill from the harbor, past the mining company's waterfront area, Two Harbors seemed awfully quiet, but as I circled the last ore dock, I saw a small pier festooned with multicolored flags. At the end lay a large tugboat, the *Edna G.* I came in alongside a barge, then tied off my boat.

"You can't moor there," a man warned.

"It's okay," I said. "I'm in town for the festival and one of your officials said I could tie up here."

"Who told you?" He looked at me suspiciously.

"One of your festival chairmen. I met him down the shore, at the Knife River marina." I was bluffing. "He suggested I stop by since this is your hundredth anniversary."

He scratched his head. "Well, okay then," he said, backing down. "Maybe the mining company is relaxing its policies during the festival."

"I think he said something like that," I said, then, changing the subject, "Is that the tug he told me about—a coal-burning one?"

"You're in luck. Captain Ojard is even on board today."

I walked over the barge to the tug. On its bridge was a large group of men, but I didn't have to look hard to figure out who was the veteran tugboat captain. He was not a tall man, nor did he wear a uniform, but by his bearing, silver hair, and steely-eyed look, he alone seemed like he belonged there.

"I'm Marlin Bree," I said, moving toward him. "I have that wooden sailing boat moored over there."

"I saw you come in. Nice-looking boat."

"This boat of yours, " I said appreciatively, "must be one of the last of its kind."

"It is," Captain Adolph Ojard said. "She's the last of the

coal-burning tugboats in this country, built in 1896. I've been with her twenty-seven years; I'm retired now and so is she. As a matter of fact, she's on the registry of national historic places—one of the few floating ones."

"A coal-burning one."

"And can she burn coal!" He warmed to his subject. "Let me tell you about the time we had to go out after the *Joe Thompson*. She lost power about eighteen miles from here, and I had to bring her in. We towed her back with her rudder cocked. By the time we got back to Two Harbors, my fireman had lost nineteen pounds."

"What? He fired it by hand?"

"Sure. She's the only hand-fired coal burner around. We always kept a hundred ton in her, with her bunkers full."

"Pardon my asking, but is steam really good to power a boat?"

Captain Ojard looked surprised. "When it comes to handling, it has diesel all beat to hell. It's faster; for example, when I want reverse I've got it. But a diesel will take you sixty seconds."

"Doesn't it take time to get steam up?"

"In the old days, we had three crews and kept the fire up at all times. By hand firing, you can boost steam up in a hell of a hurry. We could get underway in a half hour."

I looked about me, wondering. "How fast will she go?"

"Well, she's a hundred ten feet long, with a beam of twenty-three feet and a draft of fifteen feet, six inches, and her propeller is nine feet in diameter with a twelve-foot pitch. That works out to one revolution every twelve feet. At a full one-twenty-five r.p.m., which is not too slow for steam, she'll cruise at twelve and a half knots, and wear fourteen and a half knots at full speed." He paused. "Trouble is, at full speed the fireman can't keep up. She burns roughly a ton of coal an hour."

Captain Ojard glanced over the harbor to the big sea. "We didn't begrudge her anything. She got us there and back again. Let me tell you about one time in the winter we had to take her out. A fisherman went in the A.M. to tend his nets about eight miles southeast of Two Harbors. It was in January. He was gone all day, and his family got worried as night came on. He had ship-to-shore radio, but his family hadn't heard from him.

"They called me, and I got a crew together. Once we got outside the breakwall, there was quite a sea on. We fought high waves and wind; my radar didn't work in the snow-storm. I tried to figure out where he'd be and tried to reach him by radio. But every time I tried to receive his message, all I heard was a click. Finally, I figured things out and said, 'Frank, if you can hear me, click your button twice.'

"I heard two clicks. Obviously, his battery was nearly gone, not enough to transmit his voice. But we got his clicks. Now the problem became one of finding him.

"I turned on my searchlight. 'Frank,' I said, 'when the searchlight is on you, click your button twice again.'

"We swung the light, and when it was on him, I heard two clicks again; now I knew what course he was on, and headed toward him. He had been drifting all day, and as we drew near, I saw he had all sorts of garbage out as a sea anchor—fish crates, five-gallon buckets—anything to hold the bow into the wind and keep him off the rocks. Remember, we had a northeaster out there, with fifteen-foot seas, and the tem-perture was five degrees above zero.

"We worked our way up to him, and the first thing he said was, 'Nice to see you.' But that was the end of the pleasan-tries. I tried to get him to transfer over to my boat, but I couldn't take him off. He had a covered steel fishing boat and wouldn't leave her, and so he crawled up on the bow and pulled over the line that we tossed him, and we towed him in. We had found him only a few miles from a storm-swept beach."

It had been that close. Navigation could be tricky; he and his beloved *Edna G.* had gone out to rescue even big ore boats. One, the *James Farrell*, had caught a northeaster and tried to get in but couldn't and was being carried to the rocks. Despite the storm, Captain Ojard had maneuvered his tug alongside the giant ore boat and tossed up a line. But as he recalled, "By the time we got her stopped, her stern was so near rocks the propeller was kicking up sticks." That had been another close one.

"Do you sail on the lake these days? I mean, for yourself?"

"I don't own a boat. I spent all the time on one that I want to. Now, if I want to do some rocking, I'll get me a rocking chair."

I decided to wait until morning to shove off. If I left now I'd be caught somewhere along the cliffs when darkness fell. In the morning, I'd have a full day to run up the north shore.

I thought I might catch some of the festival. I locked my hatch and walked briskly away from the waterfront, up a winding, woods-shadowed road to the entrance to the mining company. Past the security office and further up the hill lay the town. I knew I was not supposed to be on mining property, nor have my boat tied up at its pier, but I figured that if I could get my visit squared away with the guards, I could probably stay overnight.

The guard at the gate was agreeable after I told him that I was in town for the festival. "I'll be back later," I said. "So be sure to let me in."

"Dock gate'll be locked," he said. "But anybody who's out to conquer Superior in a sailboat won't have any trouble getting over it."

"Over the gate?" I asked.

"Sure. Just climb up and over."

I shrugged, but as I walked past, I heard his mutter, "You won't get me out on that lake. Out there, a storm can come up fast, and you can be dead in five minutes."

Main Street lay just a few blocks above the harbor, and soaring above that were the beginnings of the north shore's mountain range. The town was festive: Flags fluttered from lampposts and some natives had dressed in their 1880s best to help celebrate the centennial of iron-ore shipments from the Mesabi Range. I was happy to be wandering among the throngs of tourists in bright sportswear.

By late afternoon the streets had emptied out and the festival adjourned for the day. I judged that the sun was over the yardarm—time for a drink—and opened the creaking screen door of the Silver Dollar saloon. In the dim light, I saw a large mahogany bar, darkened with age; the wooden floors creaked beneath my boat shoes. I felt like a prospector, hot and dusty, heading into a wild West saloon.

"I'll have a daiquiri," I announced, relishing the thought.

"All we got is beer." The elderly red-headed woman behind the bar viewed me with disgust.

"Exactly," I said quickly. "A beer."

As I drank, she pushed the screen door open and stood looking at something on the horizon, just above the nearby hill.

I looked, too. It was a huge, ominous cloud, seeming to be held back by the ridge.

"Something's coming," she finally said.

Whatever it was, I was glad to be off Superior.

In my boat that evening, the air was heavy, the atmosphere hot and sticky. This was odd weather for the waterfront; I couldn't forget the bartender's comments or the strange black cloud.

I was still wide awake at 4:30 A.M., perspiring in the sultry morning blackness, so I rolled out of my bunk and peered out my portlight at the inky, still harbor. I made a pot of coffee and turned my VHF radio to Weather 1 to check the forecast for Superior. It would be a mild day. I figured I might as well start.

I cast off my lines and slowly motored around the corner

of the ore dock. A thousand-footer had arrived and was now taking on cargo.

A man looked down from its stern high above me. He seemed to shake his head—and turn away—when he saw me wave.

I sailed past the breakwaters onto the big lake. It was chill, eerie, with patches of fog.

Hours later, I shakily retied *Persistence* alongside the barge. It now seemed like ages—an eternity—had passed. The festival's multicolored flags were fluttering in light breezes; gaily attired tourists wandered along the waterfront. A band was playing. I blinked in the glare; my clothing was plastered to my body with nervous sweat.

Slowly, I climbed up on the dock and made my way out of the mining company toward civilization. At the festive town hall, I noticed some people staring at me; I was in a daze. I walked aimlessly until I came to the newspaper office I had visited the day before.

The manager turned pale.

"You're back!"

"I found a storm," I mumbled.

"A sailboat was calling for help. I was listening to the radio; he said he had capsized three times. Was that you?"

". . . off Castle Danger . . . a northeaster caught me . . ." Shaking my head, trying to concentrate, the words came out hard. ". . . had some trouble."

She was still staring at me as I left. I realized I had given a very strange account of my last six hours on the lake. But it all rushed vividly back. I had been sailing northward, sitting in my cockpit, when terrifying events had overtaken me. Cloud banks like huge bowling balls had rolled onto the lake, water moving as I had never seen it before had piled high into racing waves that nearly took me under. The storm I had been warned against had found me, caught me with no place to hide. I had run for my life. If I hadn't spotted the entryway, I could be out there still.

Wearily, I edged my way through the crowds along the dock, then walked across the barge to my boat and fell into a deep sleep.

I had been smarter this time, I reassured myself, as I ventured out again the next morning. By leaving later, I could see how the weather was developing. Today the signs were good : there was only a light mist of fog and no hint of a rising storm. This time I stayed close to shore. *Persistence* churned along at half throttle, spray splashing from her bow as I began punching through the waves. But we were using a lot of effort. I was beginning to worry that I might not have enough fuel to make it up the shore.

I felt a cold breeze on my right cheek. As I turned my face to determine its direction, the wind seemed to intensify.

"Damn!" I swore. Out of the mist, a howling gale sprang up, and I was caught once again, but this time close to a lee shore. The savage winds and racing waters could carry me onto the waiting rocks.

I threw the tiller over, but the screaming wind tried to lever the mast down into the water.

The northeaster had returned.

I twisted the Mariner up to three-quarters throttle. As we righted ourselves, I concentrated on aiming through the racing breakers, which continually threatened to slew us broadside.

Whump! They hit on the transom and side of the boat, giving us a nasty shove. No sooner would I correct, then the breaker would roar past and we would have to get ready to take on the next one. Spurts of water gushed into the cockpit. The outboard was dipping in and out of the water, snarling nastily.

Suddenly, I looked over at the rocks. Much too close ! The

waves were catching us almost broadside, bouncing us down to beam ends.

We were in great danger. I sharply twisted the Mariner's throttle to full open.

Slowly, we began to claw away, trying to head toward the open lake. Now we cleared the rocks. I let out a sigh of relief.

The mist was thickening, and another storm seemed to be brewing. I reentered the harbor and shakily tied up again at the old barge.

Night came. The lights on the ore docks blurred in fog. It was dark and eerie on the waterfront. I pulled on a heavy sweater and parka and made my way onto the misty dock and crossed through the woods up the hill. Soon the mining company's security building loomed in front of me; I tapped the window and a surprised guard looked up.

"Glad to see you tonight," Bill Burke finally said, after he recognized me, then motioned me to the side door. "I'd heard you were back on the dock."

I slowly sipped coffee, beginning to enjoy the warmth of being inside. The guard was doing the same. Outside, there was no traffic. It was a slow evening for both of us. He had an interest in Superior, too, but different from mine. He was interested in what lay below the surface.

"Before I had a back injury, I used to do a lot of scuba diving up here," Burke explained. "In fact, I was among the first to explore the Canadian steamer, the *Emperor*. She struck Canoe Rocks off Isle Royale in 1947 and still lies in a hundred fifty feet of water, with her stern sticking out over a deep cliff. Twelve went down with her, including four women. We were the first ones really to penetrate in and we found one body."

"You actually found a body—down since 1947?"

Burke cleared his throat. "The nose was pretty well gone, the eyes were gone, but surprisingly a good part of his lips were still there ; the face, his skin, his hair, his clothes were still there, and the only thing that was truly missing—and that was a kind of a mystery and we presume it was due to the explosion of the boilers—were his arms from the elbows down. Had you known this person, and, mind you, this was after twenty-eight years on the bottom, you would have known him, for he was that well preserved."

"You didn't just leave it down there, did you?"

"We contacted a ranger at Isle Royale and he went down with us. He had a wet suit on, but that kind compresses at that depth to where it is paper thin so that there are no insulating qualities. He was not really qualified to go that deep. He got pretty well 'narced up' [problems with nitrogen narcosis—rapture of the deeps], took one look at the body—it was a pretty gory thing—and he didn't want anything to do with it."

"That kind of put you back to first base again."

"We found out that if we brought the body up, and we couldn't find anyone to take charge of the burial, we would be the ones responsible. Since the newspapers told about our finding the body, we had another problem. We were afraid the body would draw curiosity seekers, divers who weren't qualified to go that deep. We had to do something. So we finally decided to go back down and drop the body off the stern."

"In effect, off the cliff."

"Right. That should have eliminated the problem."

"Did it?"

"Well, when we went down, we took some pictures. Later on, when we were looking at the slides, we noticed that on one of the bunks, with a lot of junk on it, was another body. You could see the legs, you could actually see the formation of the hind end, and the upper body and the arms reaching up, but we couldn't see the head because it was covered."

"So there are more bodies on board? Still down there?" A shiver ran up my spine.

Burke looked at the fog over the harbor. His thoughts

seemed to be far away. "There are boats that still haven't been discovered. For example, we know that the steel freighter, the *Benjamin Noble,* sank somewhere down the shore from us because the wreckage washed ashore. The crew was all lost when she went down in 1914 and she is believed to be sunk a short distance off Knife Island."

"I came by there," I said. "Why did she go down?"

"She was overloaded. The story was that at the ore docks here, they had not enough steel for two boats and too much for one, and when they got all that in her, she was so full that her anchor pockets were actually submerged.

"Why didn't the captain refuse?"

"Those were hard times and hard men. The captain probably was worried, but he probably figured if his boat made it with someone else, he'd be branded as a coward. She made it out of the harbor, into the lake, and down to near the Duluth entryway. But a terrible storm came up and caught her. It was night, and one of the lamps marking the entryway was washed out, so the captain couldn't tell where the channel was. He had to make a hard decision, and that was to turn around to head back to Two Harbors. He didn't make it and they haven't found him yet. He and all his crew vanished that night."

"Another mystery of Superior," I said.

"There's a lot about Superior that we don't know yet, including a lot of ships that are still down there, untouched since they went down."

"I'd think the wrecks down there would be as dangerous as the dive."

"They can be. Up at Isle Royale, the water is very clear, and it's worthwhile going down. The wreck of the *America* lies up there. This diving club I was with came upon the wreck just as another boatload of divers were getting out of their diving gear and starting toward shore. Somebody started shouting: 'Where's my brother, where's my brother?' So they went back down, but they couldn't find him.

"They also didn't know the wreck very well, so they called in another diver who had a lot of experience on it. But by the time he got down, you knew the missing diver was gone and it was just a matter of finding the body. When they did, they found that the missing diver had gotten separated from his brother, had entered a room, got lost, and in panic, started flailing around and stirring up clouds of silt. He couldn't find his way back out."

Outside, mist formed on the windows and lights grew halos. "It's such an eerie feeling," Burke said slowly, "when you start down from the surface and away from your boat and all you have is this line going off below you. You pull your way down, and suddenly there looms this huge man-made thing. One old stack has this huge hole that is so big that you can just imagine something roaring up to grab you and drag you back in. You look in the old portholes, your mind gets carried away, and you imagine an old, horribly decomposed face staring back at you. Your mind races.

"Of course, the bodies are still down there. If they stay inside the wreck, protected from the fish, the body will still be well preserved. This body we found, we figured it was the engineer, but had you known the person in life, you would have known the body twenty years later. The body was still firm and surprisingly solid; I don't know if there is a petrifying process involved. We've got pictures of our divers holding the body up, one on either side. But the strange thing is that, when they opened the door in the compartment for the first time, it created a suction and we saw him kind of moving in there, lifting up and waving as if he were still alive.

"But one gal was real brave. She was studying to be an orthodontist. She went right up to him and whatever was left of his lips she peeled off and looked at his teeth. I wasn't that interested."

I cleared my throat, then switched the subject back to shipwrecks: "Isn't a ship lying out near where I'm berthed?"

"Right near the breakwater, where you entered. It's the *Ely*, a three-masted schooner that got broken on the rocks in a storm in 1896. Fascinating wreck—some of the original paint is still on the decks, that's how well preserved it is. I invited up a diver who was used to salt water, and he was amazed. He told me, in fact, that the wreck was 'fantastic,' saying how on any wreck he'd dived on in the ocean that there was practically nothing left because of the salt water's erosion. 'But here,' he said, 'I couldn't believe how good of a shape that vessel was in.'

"It's so impressive, the shipwrecks we have up here," Burke concluded happily. "It's quite a diver's paradise."

I made my way in the fog down through the woods to the wet dock and climbed on board my boat. It was dark and cold inside, but I was used to that. The shivering was from the stories I'd heard.

Opening the hatch, I paused for a moment to stare over the harbor toward the breakwater. I knew now what lay out there: below the surface was another boat, the *Ely*, all 200 feet of her.

I swallowed hard. This may well be a paradise for divers, but for the skipper of a small boat, it was altogether something else.

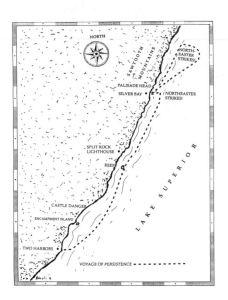

12

TRAPPED
AT
SILVER BAY

I did not realize it, but Superior was about to give me the most severe test to date. I only knew I had to push my boat hard to get to my next destination, Grand Marais, as quickly as I could.

The fog banks that had loomed like a dark headland were gone; I motored across a gentle sea, with winds so light I could not put up my sails. It was hard to believe this was the same lake I had battled only days before. But I had learned my lesson and was taking no chances.

In my battle with the northeaster days before, I had nearly run out of gasoline. I had bought an auxiliary gas tank and now had a total of 9 gallons of fuel on board, surely enough to keep me out of trouble. Or so I thought.

I drove *Persistence* past Encampment Island, Castle Danger, and Gooseberry Reefs; soon the rocky shore began to climb into the Sawtooth Mountain range. Now steep cliffs came down to the lake. I was getting deeper into wilderness country, still as primitive in areas as the early explorers had found it. I remembered the admonition of one lake captain: "It's a good thing you're not headed up the north shore later this fall; otherwise, if anything happened to you or your boat, they wouldn't find you until spring."

Not encouraging. I knew other ships had met their ends here. Off Encampment Island, for example, the *Lotta Bernard* lay in the depths somewhere beneath my keel. She had been a wooden sidewheeler that sank in the fall of 1874; three people were lost. I tried not to think about it.

The time was nearing 12:30, and I was slumping in the cockpit when I noticed something odd. The water had turned from its cobalt blue to a kind of yellow-green. How nice that the water has started to brighten up, I thought.

Suddenly, adrenaline shot through me. I yanked the tiller over. I knew why the water had turned yellow-green. I had just found a reef. I watched helplessly as we glided along and the greenish color turned even lighter. I saw the point of the reef clearly in the depths. It lay 8 feet below me; a little mountain range that grew as I turned. It was going to be a close race; would I scrape bottom or turn away first?

Worse, if I won the race, the victory might be a hollow one. I didn't know the shape of the reef; where it began or ended. I could run across another jagged point. For all I could tell I was in the center of several reefs, any one of which might tear the bottom out of the boat.

Just as the reef came to a point, I veered and the water turned blue again. In a moment, it was all over. I was back in safe, deep water.

Shaken by the incident, I checked my chart. There was a series of little stars, indicating reefs, marked not far out from Split Rock River. I had planned my course far enough off shore to avoid them, but while I was supposed to be thousands of feet off, I nearly ran aground. It was a dangerous matter—I would have to be more careful. Foregoing some of the delights of staying closer to the shore to see the scenery, I chose safety and gave myself more sea room.

The cliffs rose higher as I came to Split Rock Point and the famous old North Shore Lighthouse atop the point. The structure had been built before the turn of the century as an aid to ships in these particularly dangerous waters. Building materials had been brought in by boat and hoisted up the cliff by cable and rope while the sea dashed about below—there had been no shore road until the 1920s.

I had hoped to anchor, perhaps spend a day at this site. But as I came closer to the rocks, I could see how difficult it would be to bring a boat alongside that cliff in anything but a dead calm. There would be no protection whatever for me if a storm came up again.

I headed off, knowing that I was passing near another shipwreck, the *Madeira*. She had been a manned three-masted steel schooner barge under tow by the *William Endenborn*, a 478-foot ore freighter. In a terrible storm in November 1908, her towline parted and she crashed upon Gold Rock. One crew member somehow leaped from the deck to a cliff, carrying a rescue line with him. He threw it back to let three men escape from the bow section, and then, working his way above the broken stern section, again tossed his lifesaving line. This time five more men grabbed the lines, but one man washed overboard and died.

I looked around : Here, there was no safety. No place to run, no place to hide. The Old Commodore was right ; this was a dangerous place to get caught in a northeaster.

I turned up the throttle of my engine a bit more.

By 3 :00 P.M., I was opposite Silver Bay, a manmade harbor clawed out of the side of the rocks in 1955 by Reserve Mining Company to process and ship taconite pellets. I wondered whether these Silver Bay facilities were able to provide a safe harbor in rough weather to the huge ore boats. There would be no protection whatever from westerly storms, and only limited protection from southerly storms. In a northeaster, an ore boat would have a fight to maneuver in the harbor, let alone dock safely.

I didn't like it much and had no desire to spend time here, especially since this was a privately owned area that offered no small boat facilities. In fact, I was warned by the piloting books I carried to stay out of this harbor; it was used for commercial shipping only. I continued north.

As I neared Beaver Island, not far from the mouth of Silver Bay, I found myself among a number of small fishing boats. Some were open aluminum fishing prams, rolling their gunwales within inches of the water, while others were large fiberglass jobs. Each boat held two to four fishermen, some with poles out on either side.

There was a mystery here. My chart didn't show a marina nearby and I knew they could not use the ore boat dock, either. Where had they all come from? And why were they out here just off the breakwall?

I waved as I sailed past, but no one waved back. The north shore sport fisherman was a pretty grim sort—no one even seemed to look up. The friendliness of the south shore was definitely gone. They were a hardy lot, trusting their lives out here, but they made me feel like an interloper in their private domain.

It was now midafternoon. The day was hot and sultry; I kept to my 6¼-mile-per-hour average, and other than being tired, I saw no reason not to continue on—I'd cruise all night if necessary. My next marina was still far up the shore about 54 miles, which translated to another 8½ hours or so in this cockpit. That meant I'd arrive in Grand Marais a little before midnight. But I kept remembering the old Scandinavian adage that "he who does not sail in fair weather will have to sail in foul." I had tasted Superior's foul moods and wanted no more of them.

I passed a savage-looking set of rocks cleaving the waters like miniature mountains. Seagulls made their homes in the peaks; some flew off as I sailed past. I was glad to be sailing by now; I'd surely not want to run across them in a storm.

Ahead of me was a huge peak with steep sides, the Palisade Head. It was nearing 3:30 P.M. when I noticed that the distant sky above the rugged shoreline had a color I had come to dislike intensely: dark blue, almost purple.

I brought out my binoculars for a close-up: The mountain was holding up storm clouds; beyond, what I had thought was dark shore in shadows was a cluster of heavy storm clouds spilling out onto the lake. Quickly, I turned my craft about, looking for shelter. As I roared back along the breakwall protecting Silver Bay, I noticed something else—all the little boats were gone. I was alone.

I turned toward the mouth of the harbor and looked up at the sky. It seemed bright and clear enough, although clouds were beginning to form above the hills overlooking the bay. I stood up, trying to figure out where the boats had gone, and where I was going to find shelter. There didn't seem to be much at the dock, just concrete and steel pilings at the edge of the cliff. At one end, a huge freighter was taking on taconite.

As I rounded Beaver Island, opposite the ore docks, I saw a spit of sandy land, lying low in the water.

Any old port or island in a storm, I said to myself, swinging in. I was quite pleased with myself. I had been alert and had come off the lake before the storm hit; my track record at outwitting storms was improving.

As I explored this makeshift port, I saw the island was sort of L-shaped. The hook of the land was slender protection from the wind—little more than a low, eroded sandy beach. The main section, however, was large and rocky, with granite chunks that knifed out of the water. I'd stay away from those.

I turned my boat to head into the wind, realizing that the storm would come over the sandy beach, not the big island. No protection at all from the winds, but at least it would keep the waves from marching in.

I went on deck with my two Danforth anchors, one an 8-pounder, with 4 feet of chain on its base coupled with 5/16 braided Dacron, and the other, my "lunch hook," also a Danforth, but only of 4 pounds, attached to a 1/4-inch nylon 3-twist line. I would use both. The 4-pounder felt a little light, but it might take up some of the strain if the winds really got howling. The 8-pounder would have to do most of the work.

After I set my anchors at about a 45-degree angle to the boat, I ran my Mariner at full throttle in reverse gear. *Persistence*'s bow bobbed down. I shut off the engine. The big anchor had held. I was happy.

I moved with swiftness to check the jib, verifying that it was snugged down tight and no sheets were loose ; I lashed the mainsail to the boom, and finally looked around one last time. All was storm-ready.

Below, I put in my hatch board covers and then slammed the heavy mahogany hatch shut. It sealed with a reassuring thump. Sitting with my knees up on the bunk, I looked out a portlight at the rock-strewn shoreline not far away. Seagulls had come down to the water's edge and were looking curiously back at me.

I realized that I was in closer to the shore than I really wanted to be, but there was no time to reset the anchors. Besides, I didn't know how deep the bottom was here, and so if I wanted to anchor securely, with enough scope, I'd have to stay close to shore.

I had made my decision ; now I could only await the storm. I reached into the bilge for a can of fruit juice.

Whump! I braced myself as I felt the first unstable gusts slam into us. *Persistence* tipped a little to one side, then righted herself. Not bad at all, I thought as I had my first sip of juice.

Whoom! Whoom! Whoom! The next gusts hit in bursts of power, driving us backward. The anchor line was under a strain. The velocity of the winds was more than I had expected. I held on to my can of juice, but I wasn't drinking anymore. My throat had started to tighten up.

With a blast that thoroughly shook *Persistence*, the gale began showing its strength. I heard a terrible shrieking in the rigging ; I felt the bow straining at the anchor. We were beginning to vibrate and rattle as well. Rain pounded on the coach roof.

Suddenly, we tipped sideways. The gale now was shoving us from side to side. As the boat righted, I stole a glance out my portlight. Then I knew we had another problem. The seagulls had become much larger—I was now much closer to them and the shore.

I could see their eyes very clearly—there was a flock of them in this little cove of the island, all standing nearby at water's edge. I was fascinated by how they managed to keep from being blown away. They ducked their heads and their tails rose up high. They were using their bodies as airfoils to make the wind press them down on the sand, but even they were having trouble in this wind.

The gale rattled the furled sails and tried to bend the mast back, lifting the bow. The anchor line stretched backward. I'd feel us tremble, and then surge toward the shore.

The wind had shifted so that we were no longer being held by the big anchor, just by the little lunch hook, with the stretchy three-strand line.

I felt like a yo-yo. The wind would claw at the mast and the boat, shove us back, rattling and vibrating, twisting from side to side and up and down. We'd get within feet of the shore, and I'd begin to pray, then we'd zip forward again on the nylon line.

This was very serious. If we were to stretch back into the rock-ribbed shore, the hull would be punctured for certain. Or, if my wooden rudder hit bottom in the bouncing waves, it would break.

Perspiring and terrified, I thought of going out on deck to tighten up the anchor line, but I doubted I had the strength. In this nightmare I had little chance of doing anything useful. I'd probably only get myself hurt.

I came to only one inescapable conclusion: *Persistence* had to fend for herself, as well as for me.

The storm abated as abruptly as it had begun; the sun came out again. I threw open the hatch and reentered the day, blinking in the bright light. My friends throughout the ordeal, the seagulls, had now flown off. I was alone on this deserted spit of land.

The island wasn't much protection, and I began wondering what my next action should be. I checked my watch: it was nearing 5:30 P.M., and I still had a few hours of daylight left to voyage on up the shore. But there was nothing between me and Grand Marais but one other ore dock facility, also carved out of the side of a rock.

I trod my deck, trying to sense what the sky would do. It was muggy and hot; the droplets were beginning to dry up on the teak deck. I didn't trust the weather. It felt unstable, a lot like it had just before the storm I had run into down the shore. Or rather, the series of storms that I somehow kept nosing into. Perhaps more were coming.

I looked around. At the other end of the harbor, some distance from the ore boat, was another little boat. I pulled out my binoculars and studied it carefully. It was a powerboat of some sort, and it looked like it was tied up along the high dock, not far from a huge crane.

That gave me an idea. If one boat could sneak in alongside the mining company's private dock, well, maybe another boat could also. It was growing late, but I could quietly sail over and tie up nearby. I looked around once more; the end of the harbor was deserted. There was no one to kick me off.

I went to the bow, pulling up my anchors. They came up remarkably easily from the black, sandlike substance. I could not believe that my boat had held so well on just those little Danforths, but it had. I wiped them off and stowed them below almost reverentially.

As I glided across the quiet water to the end of the harbor, I saw that the other vessel was an all-steel powerboat, extensively equipped with electronic gear. No one was aboard. I looked up; towering above me was a huge, black crane, rusty with age. The dockside was black—this was the coal-loading area. Huge mounds of coal lay by the taconite plant, whose rusty metal buildings seemed notched into the

steep hill. There was little comfort here, and even more iso-
lation. It was as if I had landed on the dark side of the
moon.

This area was not built for small boats like mine. I put the
engine into neutral, stood up, and went to the bow; we approached a high piling that had an old truck tire hanging
down. With a mooring line in my teeth, I reached up to grab
the tire to secure us, then tied two more lines, fore and aft,
to steady the boat and ensure we wouldn't swing too far
either way. *Persistence* was balanced against this single tire.

I hoped rough weather wouldn't come up, because I
didn't know if the lines would keep us from sliding under
the projecting dock, trapping me inside.

It was eerie. As darkness fell, I saw distant lights illumi-
nate the giant boat against the dock; guard lights spotted
the dark buildings on the hill. Somewhere, deep in the earth,
there was the rumbling noise of heavy machinery.

I opened a can of stew, ate it quickly, and settled back in
my cabin, trying to relax. Outside, I heard the crunch of
boots on gravel. I worried that the guards had seen me
sneak in and were going to kick me out!

I opened my hatch; its light revealed a startled young
seaman staring down at me. "I saw your lights," he said as
he introduced himself. He was from the thousand-footer.

"I caught a little weather anchored out there," I explained. "So I came in for protection."

"Saw you out there," he said, nodding his head sympathetically. "And then you were gone. I wondered what had
happened."

He worked in the engine room. I was curious about how
such a huge boat managed to maneuver alongside this dock
by itself.

"Bow thrusters," he said. "But beyond that, I really
don't know. We're down there, but the controlling is done
from the bridge; much of our work is automatic. I usually
don't even know what the weather is like or where we are.

"And that's why I like to get out and walk—to stretch my

legs and see some weather again." He seemed terribly non-chalant about being in this remote port, about to go back upon this big sea in the bowels of the huge ship.

"Feels like another bit of weather coming in," I said looking up at the night sky. I began to worry.

"Good," he said, cheerfully. "That'll give us a lift to Cleveland." He seemed to walk jauntily back to his ship, pleased with the prospect.

I had just begun to sleep soundly when I felt something shake the boat; I sat up with a start. There was a great howling blast—the storm had returned.

The rain came in semisolid masses. The small light up on shore was now obliterated for seconds by the storm. If I angled my head just right out my forward portlight, I could barely see it. My boat hobbled about in the blackness, creaking against the single tire. I wondered if at any moment *Persistence* might break loose and wedge itself under these pilings.

It was a long, sleepless night—I was too anxious to rest. Every now and then I tried to look through my porthole at the single guard light to see if my precarious position had changed.

The light had become my personal heavenly star. I kept looking—at dawn it was still there.

Groggy from lack of sleep, I stepped out into the cockpit and I could see my breath in the dawn's crisp air. That was a bad sign: it meant the beginning of fall in the north country. Soon, very soon, the leaves would be turning red. The storms would grow in intensity. I should be off the lake.

Something crunched beneath my feet. Pieces of coal, soot, and grime lay over *Persistence*'s varnished topsides. The storm had heaped this blackness upon us.

Easing my head up to the edge of the dock, I saw that the coal yard and the mining buildings were even more grim in the morning light—a brutal and desolate landscape carved out of the mountain.

The ore boat had left sometime in the night and now I was alone in the harbor. As I pulled around the island to enter the open waters, the sea was roiling and confused.

I quickly made up the distance that I had lost the day before, journeying farther up the shore, past Palisade Head, well on my way to Little Marais. I checked my charts. In case of an emergency, my next port could be Taconite Harbor, which would offer some protection from a storm. Unfortunately, for now there were only rocky shores and above them wilderness.

I sensed trouble as more shore came into view. Ahead lay something dark and foreboding, just this side of Carlton Peak and Leveaux Mountain.

This time I didn't have to pull out my binoculars. I knew there were storm clouds piling off the mountain range onto the lake. Whatever storm the mountains had held back last night was coming out of hiding onto the open waters.

I didn't hesitate; immediately I turned to race back to Silver Bay. I didn't want to, but I had no choice. In minutes, the sun was blotted out, and in the grayness, the wind started to pick up, then to scream. The water began to growl in wave trains of graybeards, shoving *Persistence* back and forth.

I was once again running for my life. My sails were furled, my Mariner was roaring at nearly full open throttle, and my boat was twisting and careening down the waves. We were being pushed toward shore, and the waiting rocks.

I gripped the tiller with white knuckles. I could see waves crashing up on the black, jagged reefs. My heart was pounding. I knew the powerful waves were shoving me toward them faster than I realized. In a few minutes, I would be on those reefs.

I twisted the Mariner to wide-open throttle, and, offering a prayer for the small engine not to fail me, I steered away. The hull slammed and spray dashed the length of *Per-*

sistence as we began to claw away from the lee shore and the waiting rocks, gaining momentum. Finally, we were entering the harbor and heading back to the desolate mining outpost.

I was trapped and I would have to maintain a lonely vigil until the weather cleared. As I sneaked into the dock beside the coal bins, my mood matched the darkness of the shoreline. I was disconsolate at having to return without making any progress up the shore, and angry at the weather. If the day had just turned out clear like the morning yesterday, I could easily have made it to Grand Marais.

But now that port, with its sheltered bay and marina, seemed as far away as the moon. I knew I could not possibly buck the wind or those waves.

The long day deepened into night as the wind howled about me and the coal dust settled on my boat. I was so angry, tense, and depressed, it was impossible for me to eat or to rest. It was black inside my boat. Occasionally, I looked out my portlight, but all I could see was the top of the dock and, beyond, the light that kept its lonely vigil.

Persistence lurched about, bouncing up and down in the waves that were surging deep into this unprotected harbor. The rubber tire I was lashed to groaned as my ship's weight pressed against it.

I found myself dozing fitfully, trying to blot out the howling winds but listening to the groans of my berth. My thread to sanity lay here; with the groans and jerks, I knew we were still perched upon the tire. They told me we had not broken loose.

My mind drifted in and out of awareness.

In the blackness, my fear grew. How many more of those storms could my boat and I endure?

Dawn came, its leaden clouds dropping to the black seas. The winds had abated somewhat. I rubbed my red eyes as I stood in the cockpit, surveying the big lake.

Time for another try, I decided glumly. But once I got away from shore, I realized that the wind was pushing the whitecaps into my bow, again heading directly toward me.

I turned up the throttle until my Mariner snarled defiantly. But I'd roar down one wave's back, only to stick my bow into the next graybeard. We'd slam to a halt; dark water would rush up the deck toward me. *Persistence* would lift, shake herself loose, then plunge forward again, only to jam her bow into another wave.

We fought our grim little battle, my teeth clenched— somehow I was trying to push my boat on by sheer force of will. But we made no progress.

Finally, I had to give up. Timing my turn between wave crests, I swung the tiller over, nearly laying *Persistence* down on her beam end. If she had been caught by another of those waves, she could have flipped all the way over. I was lucky, and we were now heading back at full throttle.

I was trembling as I tied up at the dock. There was nothing for me to do but to spend another hateful day beside the coal bin. Above me, the rusty crane mournfully creaked in the wind.

The next two dawns I tried to fight my way out, only to be driven back, shaken and dispirited. It was hopeless to battle the lake now. In the face of the winds, I could not sail; I was using up precious gasoline. Worse, I had come close to tragedy nearly every time I was out. Had something broken, or had my engine failed, I would have been at the mercy of the sea, to capsize or be driven onto the rocks.

As I tied up again at the dock, I looked at the deserted steel boat berthed up ahead. It seemed to have taken on water from the storms and was listing badly. Worried, I began walking along the bleak embankment, looking for an office.

I saw another vessel, a large keelboat, all white with her green sail covers carefully in place. Over her cockpit was a proper dodger to shield her sailors from the wind. She, too,

was berthed at the dock; I approached carefully, and said,
"Hello!" several times. No one answered or looked out from
the drawn curtains. I felt even more alone.

Trudging in the chill wind, I clutched my parka about
me. Through the harbor entrance, I saw that the big sea was
raging, with graybeards rising up in the distance. Just the
sight of it made me shudder.

At the end of the dock, I found a small metal building;
taking a deep breath, I walked inside. Ceiling bulbs burned
dimly. A heavyset man in a khaki work shirt looked up from
his steel desk.

"I've got the small wooden sailboat," I said, introducing
myself. "But I ran into a storm and so I'm tied up at your
dock."

"That's okay," he said. "I saw your mast sticking out by
the crane. Are you all right?"

I breathed a sigh of relief—I knew I was not supposed to
be on the mining company's dock.

"I'm fine," I said, "but I noticed the steel boat in front of
me has a list. I thought I'd better walk up and report it."

"Probably the batteries that run the bilge pumps are
down," he said. "I'll have it checked out. Thanks." He
added, "We're on skeleton crew around here, so we're short-
handed."

I nodded sympathetically. Silver Bay, and the mining
company that ran it, was on hard times. Foreign steel imports had lowered the demand for ore from Minnesota's famous Mesabi Range, just north and west of here—once the
biggest iron mines in the world. Over the years, many mines
had closed.

"There's another sailboat down the wharf," I said.

"They came in this morning," the dockmaster said, now
sipping coffee from his thermos cup. "Said their boat was
doing just fine, but they weren't."

"Nice keelboat," I said, wistfully. "Big enough to handle
the waves."

"They said they'd been battling their way down the lake

and had to put in for a couple hours of rest. Then they said they'd be on their way again." He looked at me pointedly.

"I'll be on my way, too, as soon as the weather clears a little. Right now, the wind is right on my nose and the waves are kicking up. I've been out this morning, but I couldn't get anywhere."

"Well, good luck on your voyage. Let me know if we can do anything."

I felt much relieved. At least I would not be pressured to leave my safe berth. Once again, I returned to my end of the dock, unable to go up the shore, and unwilling to turn back to civilization.

That night, the dreams were bad.

I awakened, perspiring heavily, then lay back on my bunk and listened to the pounding of the water inches away. I heard the wind howl on the mast and in the rigging, and felt the creak of my boat against the old tire.

I passed the night twisting and turning in my bunk, trying to ready my mind for tomorrow and what I hoped would be my final bout with Superior.

The sun rose like a glowing ball over the lake, hurting my eyes with its rays. Off to port lay Palisade Head; once again I was on my way, climbing higher and higher along the rugged coast.

The lack of sleep was beginning to make me feel wooden. My brain seemed numbed, and my eyes hurt. I knew I'd have to be careful out here.

But once again I saw the dark clouds over the mountains ahead of me; once again I saw them sliding eerily upon the lake. I looked at my telltales switching to the northeast. I was stunned.

What should I do? I was a reasonable man, but this was unreasonable.

I felt a hot rush of self-pity. I was trying, but this was so unfair! I was low on gas, I was tired, and I had been battling this storm for nearly a week.

Somehow I could not bring myself to turn this time. I throttled back, waiting.

The onrushing waves slammed into *Persistence,* making her teeter, then came crashing back toward me with a thumping noise. Sheets of spray splashed outward from the pitching hull.

Still I did not turn. I hunched miserably in the cockpit, feeling the roiling motion of the boat, watching the weather flying toward me. I felt numb.

Whump! My boat took a nasty nosedive into a wave, then reared skyward. The graybeards were growing. I felt a hot lump in my chest and a terrible pressure as well. I sank back, heavily.

I began to shake. No! I finally screamed into the wind. Then I yanked my tiller over; we careened into a trough. We lay over on our side.

I was angry at myself, angry at the lake, angry at my failure. No! No! No! I swore, grabbing the throttle, giving the engine more power. Then I jerked the tiller over again. I began going around in circles.

Finally, a groaner reared up and splashed me hard. Cold and shivering, blue water in the cockpit floor, I had to face up to my desperate situation. At last I turned toward Silver Bay yet again.

I was shaking. My mood was black as I tied up; I had no fight left in me.

I was physically and emotionally exhausted as I trudged miserably down the dock, past the coal mounds to the dockside shack where I knew there was a telephone. Still trembling, I dialed home. I had to talk to someone.

"I'm in trouble," I blurted out to Loris, and began telling her the guarded truth. If she guessed the rest, she didn't let on.

"Let me come get you with the trailer," she offered.

"I can't give up," I said.

"We'll just get you to the next marina. That way, you can put in again," she continued, "and rest up a few days while you wait out the storms."

"I'll be looking for you," I said. With a shaking hand, I hung up the telephone.

I forced myself again to enter the open waters. I knew that the fishermen were putting in nearby, but I didn't know where. I had to find their secret quickly, before Loris arrived with my boat trailer.

There was nothing at Beaver Island, where I had anchored, but another breakwater guarded a part of the harbor on the lower side of the shore. Rounding the barrier, I saw a fishing boat. It had been on the *south* side, neatly protected from the northerly winds and waves.

"Is there a ramp near here?" I called, coming alongside the boat. But the fishermen, grimly concentrating on their sport, glanced up only briefly; I could not tell whether they had heard me. I stood on the cockpit seat, waving my arms. The fishermen now seemed intent on ignoring me.

I pulled away, heading closer to shore. Behind the breakwater, the weather seemed almost mild. The waves were moderate, and even the wind had been broken.

I throttled down to a mere idle, bobbing up and down, wondering what to do next. A steep, rocky cliff ran down the shore to the water's edge. Pines trees darkened the interior of what seemed to be a little cove.

I crawled forward to the bow, peering through binoculars, but I could see no sign of a ramp. And if I could not find one, Loris could not get the trailer in—or *Persistence* and myself out.

Desperately, I slumped back down in the cockpit seat, ignoring the fishermen. My patience paid off. Finally, one of them decided to move, and I followed.

He headed toward the rocky cliff, but then veered to the right, around some rocks, and disappeared.

I turned up the throttle, and as I rounded the rock, I saw, nestled against a steep hill, a single ramp leading to a dock. The area was heavily wooded, and there were rocks about, but it was a beautifully protected harbor.

This was the secret of the fishermen. If any storm came up on the horizon, they could race back to this cove and pull in their boats.

Now I, too, could escape.

My next stop would be up the shore at Grand Marais, a safe berth. At last I would get some proper rest.

13

WILDERNESS AT ISLE ROYALE

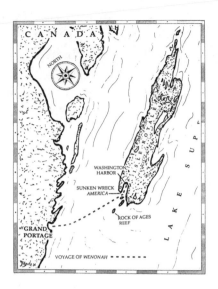

I WAS ON MY WAY TO ONE OF THE MOST MYSTERIOUS AND primitive islands on Lake Superior. I should have been glad to be aboard this vessel, the *Wenonah,* an excursion boat out of Grand Portage, in the company of the veteran Lake Superior pilot, Captain Stanley Sivertson, on one of the last of his voyages this season to Isle Royale. But instead, I felt tired and reflective. *Persistence* was now resting on her trailer in a farmyard high atop the Gunflint Trail, near Grand Marais, and I was here.

White fog engulfed the ship. Through the misted windows of the ship's bridge, I could make out the bow of the steel vessel and the cold, glassy waters of Superior—visibility was poor, only perhaps 50 yards. Though the *Wenonah* was doing about 6 knots, time seemed suspended by the fog. We floated halfway between water and air.

At the wheel, Captain Sivertson squinted into the fog bank; First Mate Dwayne Lhotka concentrated on the radar's eerily glowing green screen, now set for far range. Its concentric electronic rings spun out into nothingness, save at the far edge, where its beam outlined, and then held for a few glowing moments, the mass of the island.

It was a gray day outside and my mood matched the weather. My mind flashed back to the frustrating retreat I had made from the big lake.

It had been nearly dark before I was able to ease *Persistence* onto her trailer from the chilling waters that had nearly done us both in. I wanted to find out what damage she had suffered during our ordeal. In the fading light, with my fingers to her hull, I first felt, then saw that she had lost nearly all of the paint marking her waterline and even some of her varnish. I shook my head in dismay.

After my frantic telephone call, my family had driven nonstop to get me; I knew both of them were weary. Bill was huddled in the backseat. "Hurry up!" Loris called from inside the car. "It's getting cold."

I was shivering, too, in wet deck shoes and sopping trousers. But there was no time to change. Hurriedly, I started the car and then we climbed the winding road up to the north shore highway.

I had planned to push hard past the coastline where I had been storm bound, then slip *Persistence* back in the water at Grand Marais's small marina. But we had arrived at nearly midnight, so I parked and we clambered inside to snuggle down in our bunks. *Persistence* became an overnight camper.

Loris and Bill, tired after their long journey, fell asleep almost immediately. But I could not relax. Thoughts of storms still ran through my mind as I drifted off, waking me up, shivering in a cold sweat.

The next morning, Superior was leaden colored with a tomblike sky overhead. My enemy, the storm, had still not gone away. I walked to the water's edge and peered out. Graybeards were everywhere. Wave trains slammed into the rocks, spitting white water high.

I argued with myself. If I could find a berth, I'd be able to wait out the storm, rest up, and get some momentum going again. But when I stopped by the small marina office, I was told there was no space for my boat.

Dejectedly, the three of us began walking along the shore. Each wave that slammed upon the rocks now seemed to hit inside my head. I felt the blows.

"That's it!" I said in a voice so low Loris almost didn't hear it. "I'm giving up."

"What about your plans?" Loris was startled.

I turned my back but heard my son explain to his mother: "Dad is just depressed."

"You've come a long way," Loris said soothingly. "It's a pity to give up now."

"I know. But I can't continue."

"Perhaps you should rest and think things through when you feel better."

"Where can I go? There's no place to put in, and I just feel awful."

She began walking up the trail. "All right," she said, finally. "We'll just turn around and go back."

I found myself frowning. Now it was so simple; all I had to do was get in the car, still with the trailer and boat on behind, and drive home. Back to the green grass of what remained of summer in Shoreview; back to a world that didn't churn, where storms didn't flash out of the north, where dark seas didn't reach up to claim me. Where I would be safe. The thought tempted me.

I stopped. "I just can't give up."

"Well, what *are* you going to do?" she demanded.

"I'll find a place to park my boat on its trailer for a few days," I said as quickly as I thought it out. "I'll go on ahead to scout the shoreline. And when the storms blow out, I'll come back for her." I was gripped by a new feeling of resolve.

Now guided by the green eye of radar, *Wenonah* penetrated the edges of one of the most mysterious of the big sea's worlds. Isle Royale was an isolated 210-square-mile island far off the shore, a last unspoiled refuge for wolves and moose; to me, it was the north woods primeval. Many ship-wrecks lay on the island's sunken reefs; ancient Indians had come here to mine copper so pure it had startled the world. A tiny Norwegian fishing village had once clung tena-ciously to its tip, but that was gone. A few hardy visitors ventured to the island each summer; the National Park Ser-vice kept several rangers here. But for the most part, Isle Royale was wilderness.

"We're in the channel now," Captain Sivertson announced.

The world was silver. I peered into the fog, but I could see nothing.

"We've got to ease our way in," the captain said calmly. "We need to get past a sunken wreck, the *America,* and squeeze by the other channel. Maybe if you look out, you can see something."

I stuck my head out the window and felt mist on my face and on my glasses. But nothing else seemed to be out there.

"Up high," the captain commanded.

I craned my head, then almost ducked.

Suddenly, I saw the pine tree—its upper branches peeked out above the fog. It looked like it was right on top of us.

"That *is* close," I uttered respectfully, as the *Wenonah* glided through the rocky gorge.

"We're entering Washington Harbor, bound for Windigo Station," the captain announced proudly.

We had run out of the cottony fog bank and emerged into incredibly bright sunshine and blue skies. Inside the Isle Royale harbor, summer had returned and it felt odd to be warm again. I was dazzled.

As we made dock, the few hardy end-of-the-season pas-sengers began loading up their knapsacks, tents, and hiking equipment.

"We'll be here for several hours," Captain Sivertson warned me as we docked. "So be back by the time we sail, or elese you'll have to spend the night on the island."

I stepped out on the wooden dock and looked about.

Ahead lay a ranger station, and I walked toward it. I noticed that my nights of sleeplessness were catching up with me; I was beginning to fall asleep almost on my feet.

But then I remembered that wolves, an endangered species, inhabited this island. I hurried on.

"Threatened and endangered," Bruce Reid, of the National Park Service, confirmed. "Their largest concentration in the continental United States is on the north shore."

"Why study them on this island then?"

"You fly the north shore of Minnesota and see a wolf, and the wolf hears a plane, and he's gone," the ranger explained. "But a flying researcher can circle a pack for twenty or thirty minutes after the wolves on the island hear him. As long as you don't get to a threshold altitude where it becomes an annoyance to the wolves, they'll go about their business. Here they've never been hunted or pursued; they just don't have experience in dealing with man."

"They're on this island . . . and so are campers," I said. "Have you ever felt threatened?"

"Never even seen one!"

"They stay that much out of your way?"

"You can walk down any of the trails in this park, and you will see wolf tracks or their scat [droppings]. They're here, but they avoid us as much as we would avoid them."

"They keep that far away?"

"Visitors, and those of us who are here the bulk of the year, rarely see a wolf, except in winter. I have yet to even hear the wolves howling, but maybe I sleep too sound. They have been heard here in the Windigo area this summer, but I guess I didn't wake up in time."

I liked the thought that he slept so soundly. I hoped someday I could resume the habit.

I thanked him, then began walking along the trail leading to a camp. There were no automobile roads, or automobiles, only hiking trails.

I glanced at my watch: I still had a little time. I hoped I'd get my energy back with some exercise. I was terribly drowsy, and, to my drooping eyelids, "the royal island" seemed almost unreal in its lush vegetation. It seemed like, well, a south sea island paradise.

I was not surprised, then, when I saw an island princess coming down the trail.

She was nine or ten years old, I'd guess, with long blonde hair, and lived on the island with her family; she said she was the daughter of the ranger. She made it clear that this was her domain, but that she welcomed me to it and would show me about. I was utterly captivated and charmed.

Fearlessly, she plunged ahead up the trail, to the campsite, and I followed. It was idyllic, one of the most beautiful campsites I had ever seen. Within the island was a lake surrounded by trees. Something moved.

"Probably a moose," my young guide said.

I looked closely, but I couldn't make it out. "Ever see one?"

"A couple of times. Once campers saw them from afar. Were they ever pleased!" she said, delighted at the thought.

"Are you?"

"Oh, yes. I love to see the animals here."

We walked on; she talked and I listened mostly. I was amazed at how at ease she was on her island. She pointed out some wild berries, then offered me one; she showed me wooded campsites and told me about families that came here, to her island, just to get away from things.

When the whistle of the *Wenonah* sounded from afar, she carefully saw me back to the dock.

"Thank you so very much," I said, perhaps with too much feeling. She shrugged her little shoulders, then looked slightly embarrassed.

As she walked away, she turned once to wave shyly at me. I would miss her. She had been my special guide to Isle Royale and I realized I had relaxed more in her presence than I had in days.

I decided, then and there, that every royal island ought to have a princess, even an uncrowned one in blue jeans.

It was time to head back to the mainland. The *Wenonah* cruised cheerfully in the sunlight toward the fog bank.

"Look closely at the water," Captain Sivertson said.

We were now in the channel, but as I peered down, I couldn't make out anything. The water was clear for a number of feet. Then I saw a long black shape looming beneath the surface of the green.

"That's the *America*," Captain Sivertson said, turning his boat closer, slowing the engines.

I looked at the huge hull and shivered. We were nearly on top of her. I could make out some of her plates.

The captain began to talk about this lost boat as if it had been a friend. Her end had come abruptly, and totally unexpectedly, the morning of June 7, 1928.

He had been on the island for summer fishing, along with his sister, brother, and uncle. His father and mother were coming over on the *America*; he planned to meet them at the harbor.

"So we got up at one o'clock," he began, "but it was pitch dark when the boat came into the island dock. My dad was on crutches; we didn't know it then, but the doctor had warned him not to go to Isle Royale at all. He figured my dad would not be able to get around on the dock or in and out of the rowboat we used to get to our cabin about a half mile away. My dad took one look at the gangplank—it was wet and steep—and he decided he'd stay on the boat. The *America* was going on up to Thunder Bay, then come around Isle Royale, and he'd be by at about six o'clock in the evening. Well, we went home and back to bed. We didn't know any more until we heard my father calling us, as if in a nightmare. 'The *America* is sinking, the *America* is sinking.'

"I ran out and I saw my dad. Despite his broken hips and casts, he had somehow gotten into a lifeboat, rowed across a mile to our fishing place, and woke us up. I got into one boat and my Uncle Chris and my brother, Arthur, got into another, and we went out to the *America*; at first sight, we thought nothing was wrong. The bow was right up against the reef, and when we got a quarter of a mile away, I said, 'It doesn't look like it's sinking to me; it's just sitting there.' Then I saw the boat roll over. I saw the skylights over the engines and all the windows in the passenger staterooms blow out, just like geysers, just like fountains, when she rolled over and went down.

"It had taken about an hour for her to go down and the only casualty was a dog that belonged to a doctor. One of the doctor's kids wanted to go back, but the captain wouldn't let him: 'Don't go back to save that dog, because your dad wants you more than he wants that dog.'"

Captain Sivertson looked deeper into the water. "I was so shocked at the sight of her sinking that this was the last thing I could ever remember of that night. I don't even remember how my mother got to shore, or whether she was in the lifeboat with my dad."

The powerful engines of the *Wenonah* came to life and Captain Sivertson eased his vessel past the wreck. I saw what remained of the *America* fade in the dark waters, finally covered by the fog. Soon we were rolling in the increasing, and confused, swells.

"What happened after that?"

The captain smiled as he remembered. "Once the boat had settled, and a diver had gone down and taken the safe off, we went out there with long pipe poles to the front gangway to see if we couldn't find some trunks and suitcases or whatever. We got some, but a neighbor had rigged up a sixty-five-foot-long pole, and he snagged our family trunk. That was valuable, too, for my mother had all her keepsakes in it from Norway. So we got that back.

"But the *America* was also carrying a big cargo of fresh fruit for Thunder Bay, Ontario, and all that fruit was in wooden crates. We fished for cases of oranges, cantaloupe, grapefruit, watermelons, strawberries, grapes, and bananas. We never had it so good.

"We'd make up pails full of lemonade; we'd have strawberry shortcake and banana cream pie. One island family had a little house just about full of bananas. The funny thing was, when you were on the wreck digging out fruit, once you freed one box, a whole lot more would pop up, and they all floated. We thought we fished most of it out, but one night we got a real squall, and the next morning about twenty cases of fruit floated up along the shore by our dock, which was about a mile away. It was fantastic. All we had to do was walk down and pick out the kind we liked. The cold water kept it pretty well, too."

Captain Sivertson had remained on the island, part of a small community of Norwegians that lived in a fishing village there. I wondered what kinds of boats the old-time fishermen used.

"In the old days we used twenty-foot-long wooden boats, covered only by a removable canvas spray shield, but otherwise as open as they could be because you had float hook lines going all over. The more open the boat was, the better. But that didn't make them seaworthy, because if you had a big breaker, sometimes you could get them on board and they could swamp you.

"The open boats were cold, too. I remember one day I fished three hundred hooks, which is not a lot, but I was going up to the north side and spray would come over, and as I baited the hooks I could actually see icicles forming on my fingernails. It was pretty cold with bare hands."

"Ever think there might be a better line of work?"

Captain Sivertson shook his head. "I remember as a youth talking with this guy and saying, 'Oh boy, I'd like going out on the open water, taking on those seas with all those waves flying over the boat.' I remember he told me, 'Wait until you get older and you'll lose your zest for that.' He was partly right. But later on I gave up my open boat for a covered boat like those fish tugs they got around Bayfield. I missed the sun."

"With all those wrecks out there," I said, "why didn't somebody try to raise one?"

"At one time they did. There were some amateur divers that tried to raise the *America* back in 1966 or 1967. I heard that someone bought the salvage rights to the *America* for two hundred dollars, and one diver worked for a season to get her ready. When he returned the next season, someone had dynamited her bow and opened up her seams so that no one could get her afloat. Now she just lies there."

"Why would anyone want to do that?"

"It was done by people who wanted her where she lay. Now she's protected by the National Park Service as a historic site."

We plunged ahead in the fog now; I excused myself to walk along the rail. The few passengers on board were quiet, and I saw they were for the most part sun-bronzed campers coming back from their stay in the island wilderness.

Soon we were nearing harbor, and as I peered into the clear water, I saw we'd reached a shallow area—the reefs were a lot closer to the onrushing keel than I wanted them to be. Then I saw the wooden dock in the distant mist, and beyond that, the replica of the seventeenth-century fur trading fort with its pointed wooden stockade. The voyage was over; we were back to land.

I watched the passengers rapidly disembark from the *Wenonah* and walk down the gangplank. Soon only Captain Sivertson and I remained on board.

"Doesn't it get awfully lonesome out here?" I asked, looking out at the enveloping fog and pulling my parka closer.

"No," he said, perhaps with more finality than he was feeling. "I have my diesels to look after."

I felt the lake's cool breath on my face.

Captain Sivertson shook his head a little sadly. "This is my home," he said. "I don't leave."

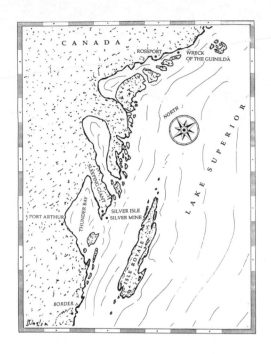

14

TO THE GOLD COAST

I WAS MESMERIZED BY THE LAND AND SKY SWIRLING around me on the Queen's Highway. I had followed Superior's mountain range, sped by island chains, and then crossed into Canada; I skirted around Thunder Bay, sped past the Sleeping Giant, and now began climbing eastward around the big lake. My destination for the night was the old Canadian fishing village of Rossport, Ontario.

I was still traveling by car. *Persistence* was landlocked and I was continuing with my plan to scout ahead, to see Superior by shore as best I could and wait for the big lake to settle down.

There was much to see. A gold strike had been reported in a moose pasture; the rumors were that it was a big one—I felt a little like a modern-day Jack London in search of new gold fields. It was not the first time that Superior's minerals had caught the headlines. Somewhere on this shore was a deserted silver mine that was once the richest in the world.

I drove hard—time was running out on me. Soon the big lake would be turning wild with the winds of fall.

As I looked out my automobile window, I could see clouds scraping against the pine-clad mountains of the Canadian shield. On one side was sky ; the other sloped downward to a rock-hewn shoreline and Superior's pounding surf. Round, rugged islets, with high, sloping sides dotted the shoreline.

It was all very scenic ; I was comfortable. Yet I felt curiously isolated, removed from the reality of the big lake. I knew that would change shortly. I still had a sailboat voyage to complete.

Below me was the blue Rossport harbor, encircled by tall islands carpeted with pines. It was as picturesque a harbor as I had ever seen, set in the folds of a hillside. If I had come by boat, perhaps I would have caught its true spirit. But by automobile, I felt like a tourist.

Partway down the steep hillside road, I began looking for an old railroad inn. Soon, off to my right, I could see it jutting up on top of an embankment, beside a clear stream, not 50 feet away from the railroad tracks.

Originally built in 1884 as a railroad hotel and pay station by the Canadian Pacific Railroad, the Rossport Inn showed its lineage in its rock foundation and rugged timber construction—I knew it had seen a lot of history.

This was Superior's wild and remote north side. "When you're out on the lake around here," Ned Basher told me, "and stop on one of the islands, you feel like you're Robinson Crusoe. If you found another footprint, you'd be surprised."

I didn't doubt him. Basher lived here as the innkeeper, a gentle man in his late thirties, with dark hair and an open grin that belied his jet jockey days. He was from New York, but while in the air force had flown over the area and fallen in love with Rossport and the old inn. Since then he had bought it, cleared out decades of accumulated dirt from the Canadian wilderness, sanded 100-year-old maple floors down to their original lightness, and was bringing the inn back to life.

Basher and I stood on the balcony, peering out over the harbor and the nearby islands. A carefully mowed patch of grass beside the railroad track immediately below me caught my eye. It was a small area of green among the wild grasses and flowers of this old fishing village.

"The Canadian railroad system is quite accommodating," Basher explained. "They drop off fishermen, canoeists, and campers at all points along the system, and will pick them up a week or so later by prior arrangement. The train goes by here twice a day—the patch of grass qualifies as our loading ramp."

Inside I paused before an old photograph of a large ship, with its bow sticking up out of the water at an odd angle, as if teetering on a rock. "That's the *Gunilda*," Basher said, and he began to tell me a remarkable tale of Superior, a millionaire's yacht, and the Rossport Inn.

Toward the end of August 1911, the *Gunilda* had been steaming in these isolated Canadian waters. The sleek steel-hulled yacht was the pride of fabulously wealthy William L. Harkness, one of the original partners of Standard Oil, who had objected to paying $25 for a local pilot to guide them into Rossport's harbor. Harkness decided to have his own captain bring him in.

Suddenly, the 195-foot yacht rammed her keel hard on a hidden reef, and continued forward, her bow sliding out of the water—stranded. Harkness, his crew, and passengers got off.

"Its bow was high, but its stern was close to the water, nearly swamped," Basher said. "Harkness called Thunder Bay to have a tug come pull him off. When the salvage tug arrived, the captain worried—he wanted to go back to bring two barges to tie on either side of the *Gunilda*'s stern to ensure stability when pulling the boat off the shoal.

"But this Harkness fellow, probably feeling that since he was in a foreign country he might get taken or something, told the tug captain to forget about the barges and to attempt to pull his boat off just the way it was. The tug captain ran a hawser completely up around the bow of the *Gunilda*; but, as a precaution, he also ordered his men to stand by with axes to cut the thick rope if the *Gunilda* should start to sink so it would not pull his tug under.

"Sure enough," Basher said, "when they started to pull the *Gunilda* off the shoal, the stern did go under—and it kept going. The tug cut its hawsers, and down the *Gunilda* went to the bottom."

He shook his head. "It now sits in about two hundred fifty feet of water out there in Lake Superior without a hole in it. It's a magnificently built boat with beautiful fittings, gold leaf on the bow, and even three grand pianos on board, so you can imagine what a two-hundred-foot private yacht built in those days must look like on the interior. Jacques Cousteau was here several years ago with the *Calypso*. They sent their submersible down just to see what it was like, and according to them, it was the most magnificently preserved wreck they'd ever seen."

"Someone now owns the boat?"

"Someone from Thunder Bay bought the salvage rights. I think that in the not-too-distant future there will be an effort to raise the yacht because it certainly is a beautiful boat, and historic, too. There aren't many yachts left from that era. This one's in mint condition. It was only two years old when it sank, and doesn't have a hole in it."

"What did Harkness do after he watched his boat sink?" I asked.

"He had a party here at the Rossport Inn," Basher said. "I suppose about all you can do after you sink a million-dollar yacht is get drunk and call Lloyds of London to tell them what they just lost."

"Must have been sad to lose that boat."

"Harkness had the last word," Ned said with a grin. "As he left, someone was grieving over the *Gunilda*. 'Don't worry,' Harkness replied, 'They're still making yachts.'"

I stayed the night at the Rossport Inn, but the next morning, Superior's north shore wilderness lay ahead of me. I had a problem. "How do I find Hemlo?" I asked.

"The gold strike is just down the highway."

"I checked my map. Hemlo is not marked."

"As you go down to Marathon, look on the left-hand side of the road, and you will see a development. It might be difficult getting in, but there are some big structures."

I hoped no glint of gold fever in my eyes betrayed me. I wondered what I would find. Perhaps the days of Robert Service lived again in this north country—feverish activity, prospectors with pans. Gold pokes bulging with dust. Dance halls, old saloons, gambling houses. Dangerous dreams, painted wimmin.

I was anxious to be gone. But the kindly innkeeper drew me aside with a caution: "A lot of people are interested in prospecting up here, so be careful."

"What do you mean?"

"You might hear some very imaginative stories."

I met him, appropriately enough, at the waterfront. He wore red suspenders and heavy boots, although I could see they were rubber, not the leather lace-up jack pine type. He was tall and thin, somewhat gimlet-eyed, an austere if not natty dresser in his green wool timber cruising trousers tucked in the tops of his boots and his salmon-colored underwear peeking from the throat and rolled-up wrists of his flannel shirt. Its stains indicated it had seen better days long ago.

He had been in the wilds of Superior for months. Certainly, with his grizzled beard and long white hair, he had not seen the inside of a barber shop for some time. I judged he might possibly be a veteran of the gold fields. I had another swig from my bottle of beer, then inquired.

"Yah. I am geologist," he said.

Perhaps it was the smoke-filled waterfront saloon; perhaps it was the lateness of the hour. I looked at him carefully—he did not look like a geologist to me.

"You know vat iss here?" He looked about, his keen north woods eyes shifting about the barroom scene. "Gult!"

"What?" I asked, startled.

"Yah, iss troo!" His eyes gleamed as he warmed to his topic. "Huntsful und huntsful . . . gult!"

His eyes glanced around the room once more, as if to see if anyone had overheard. None apparently had, so he continued in a low voice, "Eye haf found zee lost gult mine."

I remembered Ned Basher's admonition. "How did you find the lost mine?"

"I study zee satellite photography. Zen I find zee mine."

I recovered sufficiently. "You actually found gold nuggets?"

"Yah." He obviously sensed my reluctance to believe him and carefully added: "I sent zee sample to zee government, und to mining companies." He had another sip of beer.

"What did they say?"

"Gult!"

"Right here? In this area?"

His eyebrows knitted together suspiciously. "Ach! I am not divulging."

I had another swig of beer; he did the same. I tried another tack. "How big are the nuggets?"

"Beeg!" he swore, holding the palms of his hands open. "Huntsful und huntsful."

"Where are the nuggets now?" I asked.

"I half dem hidden."

"Does anybody know about your find? The mining companies that surveyed this area, for example?"

"No!" he roared, shaking his head adamantly. "Und nobody iss going to know, if dey don't come up with zee money."

That was a new development. "What are you asking?"

"Maybe hundred million."

I coughed. "That's a lot of money."

"Iss lot of money, but iss a lot of dough aftervard, too" he rationalized.

"What do you figure the yield might be?"

"Bigger than South Africa, second to none."

"That's fantastic."

"Or even maybe first to none!"

I walked dizzily into the night. Below me, the surf boomed. I had met my first prospector. I wondered what Jack London would have done.

It was late in the day when I pulled into a roadside café. I tried to envision a gold rush, but as I drove the highway along the shoreline, I had seen no prospecting going on, or, for that matter, grizzled old prospectors feverishly panning for gold. In fact, this wild area of the Canadian north shore seemed almost deserted.

The small, dark-eyed waitress bustled over. Her name was Elna, she told me, and she had lived here all her life—since the time when this was a moose pasture.

"Didn't you know that there was gold here?" I inquired.

"No." She shrugged. "Did you?"

I thought for a moment, then decided to press on. "What actually happened? Did somebody pan for gold and one day there it was?"

"No, nothing like that," Elna replied with a smile, leaning forward on the counter. "The mining company suspected there was gold, then checked into it—and so they just happened to find the largest gold strike in North America."

"And now everybody's got gold fever," I concluded, hoping to get a new grip on the conversation.

"No one's really feverish here," she said, wiping off the counter. "Not even lukewarm."

I pulled out my ace in the hole: a wrinkled newspaper clipping.

GOLD! CRY ARISES FROM SUPERIOR'S NORTH SHORE, the headline in the *Minneapolis Star and Tribune* had said last fall. I had read the story, then carried the clipping with me on the *Persistence*—and now to the gold fields.

I showed it to the suddenly interested waitress: "Estimates to be worth more than five billion dollars. . . .

gold rush. . . . Prospecting fever spreads . . ." I sat back expectantly.

"Here?" she sniffed, almost incredulously. "You mean, with the donkeys, and the pans, all over the countryside?" She laughed. "No, no! Today it's all highly mechanized, with lots of technical people, lab work, and mining specialties.

"Mining today involves mostly little specs in the ore," she explained patiently. "It takes tons and tons of ore to make a pound of gold, or something like that, and loads of technology. It's not something you can just pick off the ground."

I was disappointed and perhaps it showed, for Elna continued to enlighten me.

"Some friends from the café went down into the mine. The mining company decided to show it to the townspeople."

I became alert. This would be real news—a report from inside a modern gold mine. "What did they find?" I asked.

"Black," Elna said. "It was pitch black down there. When they shined a light around, they just saw little bitty specs in the ore."

She leaned over with a low laugh. "How about a refill on that coffee, and got any more good newspaper clippings?"

I pressed on, but wondered if I had missed the gold fields. Then, off to the north, I saw a huge, brightly colored collection of structures—they looked like part of a North Sea oil rig that had been transplanted. Driving up to the Tech-Corona Mine, I met Denis Lanteigne, who had been a gold miner before he became a security guard.

"Down around twenty-six hundred feet," he told me, "it's rather cold, about freezing, and damp. You see with a little light on your battery-powered cap. It's actually pitch black and there's no other light source around; you feel like you're blind. If you turn out your lamp and stand in the dark, you start to lose your balance and fall over."

"What's the gold like? Do you pick chunks out of the walls?"

"Here it's very minute traces. I've heard that the percentage of gold per ton is approximately from seventeen one hundredths of an ounce up to thirty-two one hundredths of an ounce per ton in this area."

I tried to imagine how little gold there actually was—a fraction of an ounce per ton—and wondered how they found gold in such microscopic quantities.

"They take core samples horizontally or vertically, like a slice of cheese, and they analyze it. It's very accurate: they know where the gold is, in what quantity, and how to get it. They can pretty well pinpoint the vein, within a reasonable margin."

"How does a miner know where to dig?"

"They tell you to go straight where you're going, up or down, or turn left sixty degrees."

"But you can't tell—you can't even see the gold?"

"It's too small. It doesn't reflect in the light and you can't see it in the rock."

This all seemed rather odd to me. "How rich is the Helmo field?" I inquired.

"One-third of the world's gold production," he said, proudly.

It went against my grain to realize that it was in such microscopic pinches, a person couldn't even recognize the stuff. Matters got even worse when I had asked how to recognize gold and was told that I had passed right by a large outcropping of gold-bearing rock by the highway.

All that glitters is not gold, I reminded myself, except that today, even gold does not glitter. It lies there in tiny dark spots in rocks, and you've got to break up 2,000 pounds of rock to get out just a quarter of an ounce of the precious stuff. High tech.

The romance and glory of prospecting was gone, I mused,

as I drove along a twisted, heavily wooded road near the Sleeping Giant mountain that guarded Thunder Bay.

Silver Islet would be my last stop by car. I was about to look into another Superior legend—the abandoned island of silver. But given my experience so far, I wondered what I'd really find. I stopped at a small old house overlooking a rocky, blue bay encircled by pine-clad islands.

"It's about a mile offshore," Ann Drynan said rather casually. "It's pretty much the way they found it back in 1867, except that there are two trees and some bushes on it now. And that's all that's left."

I peered through the window, but I could not see the mysterious island I had long heard about. She assured me that if I were to walk down the road, and look out past another island, I would see Silver Islet—the rock that held the underwater remains of the mine.

Ann had summered in this remarkable village with her family since she was a young girl, and though its mining days were over, she had known some of the original miners and had become the islet's resident historian. Now she began telling me the story of what once was the richest and most unusual silver mine in the world.

In July 1868, Thomas MacFarlane, a mining engineer, had come to survey this north shore wilderness in a steam launch with his party of seven. The area was owned tax free by the Montreal Mining Company, but the Canadian government would shortly be levying a two-cents-an-acre tax on it. MacFarlane's task was to determine which of the several thousands of acres around Thunder Cape were worth keeping.

One of his men had rowed out to a small offshore island to set up a survey marker. The island was an unimpressive hunk of rock, about 90 feet across, and 8 feet at its highest, polished smooth by Superior's storms. Because it resembled the top of a head, he named it Skull Rock. But when one of the surveying team tapped a pick into the rock to put down a survey stake, he exposed a curious black mineral, tinged with color.

"A solid vein of silver," Ann told me. "They scrambled out in the water and dug and dug—they were very excited."

The engineer and his men blasted the rock with powder and, with pickax and crowbars, tore chunks of silver from the newly found vein. What they saw when they followed the vein into the icy water took their breath away: almost pure silver, buffed bright by storms.

"This was an unusual find from the beginning," Ann said, "for it was large bodies of nuggets. They practically pried pure silver out of the rock."

The silver lode was 20 feet at its widest, running from the rock into the lake. "Problem, of course, was getting to it," Ann went on. "There was all that silver, but it was under Superior."

I could imagine the miners splashing into the water, attempting to reach the silver that lay just beyond their grasp; I could also imagine them floundering back on the rock, teeth chattering, turning blue with the icy water. They could only have worked minutes at a time.

Open to the wide sweep of Superior from every direction except the north, the tiny rock was bombarded by waves during storms and fair weather alike. The first step had been to build a reinforced structure around the projected mine, but Superior quickly tore that away. A new one was built, this time reinforced with a shield of heavy logs, but again, the big lake dislodged the shield, flooding the shaft. Even when the lake was calm, fissures in the rock would pour icy water into the fledgling mine.

When the lake froze, the miners cut holes in the ice, dropping blasting powder into the silver vein, then picked up the dislodged ore with long-handled claws. During that winter, exposed to Superior's howling winds and in temperatures that dipped to arcticlike 40 degrees below zero, they brought up about 8 tons of ore.

The mining company could tell that it had an incredible find, but after a year of failed attempts to build a shaft, they decided to sell the potential mine. Europe was wild with stories of Superior's mineral riches, but no one wanted to invest money in a rock in the lake, even though its ore was the richest ever found. Wresting the metal from the grasp of Superior was regarded as impossible.

Finally, an American industrialist, Alexander Sibley, paid Montreal Mining $225,000 for Silver Islet and the surrounding area. With this purchase, he undertook one of the most remarkable battles of man against the big sea. Sibley knew that to wrest the silver from the tiny islet, he would need the boldest mining engineer he could find. Captain William Bell Frue, a descendant of miners from Cornwall, England, had built an awesome reputation in Superior's rich copper mines on the south shore and seemed the ideal person for the job.

Frue arrived by boat in 1870 and saw that the small islet—about the size of a house—presented an enormous challenge. A careful planner, he built a rock pile 6 feet high on the islet and then climbed to the top to study the lake's action. As he sat there, a violent storm came up from the unprotected southeast; to his horror, he watched Superior's giant wave trains build and march toward his tiny rock pile, slamming into his observation post, leaving him stranded. His assistant on shore could not get a rowboat out to rescue him, and the mining engineer could only hang on, wet and cold, until the blow abated.

He began to devise his plans. As the fall winds swept the lake, he brought up a steamship, the *City of Detroit*, with a handpicked crew of thirty men, largely former tin miners from England, as well as two horses, machinery, and supplies. A scow in tow behind contained 20,000 square feet of heavy timbers, intended to become the fortress that would protect the mine from Superior.

The season was growing short. Frue needed to build a breakwater around his mine as well as to construct a village on the shore to house his miners and their families, who would arrive by boat for that first winter, which was only months away.

The desperate battle began. The captain and his crew worked every available hour to establish their mine and their wilderness post. Frue's plan was to construct a break-wall of giant timbers held by iron shafts 2 inches thick. Rock and waste, hauled by hand, filled up the inside areas of the timbers.

By late October, the islet was protected by its fortress, which stood 6 feet high atop the surface of the rock. As an additional protection, Frue built a stone and cement coffer-dam that guarded the mouth of the shaft. In the waning hours of the fall, everyone on Skull Rock worked madly toward one common goal—keeping Superior at bay.

But a storm came out of the northeast, slamming into the fortress, and waves began to overrun the breakwall. Work-ers abandoned the rock as its protection was pounded apart. That night from the mainland, Frue could only peer into the darkness at his besieged fortress. By morning's light, he had his answer: the big sea had won.

When the storm waters subsided, Frue rowed out to see that Superior had demolished 200 feet of breakwater, torn open the cofferdam, and filled the mine shaft. The 2-inch-thick iron rods had bent like wire.

Desperate, Frue rebuilt his fortress stronger and bigger than before, with the crib now extending out 26 feet. He sank his first mine shaft from the surface into the depths of Superior, down past solid rock. Later, in his small shack, he assayed his mine's ore. It was richer than even the fabulous Comstock Mine—the greatest yield of silver per ton ever known!

At the end of November, as the cold north winter set in, a storm arose out of the southwest. The big lake churned up ice floes like battering rams. All night long, the miners could hear the ice masses grinding across the fortress, tear-

ing away the cribbing. Somehow, the cofferdam had sur-
vived : the mine shaft was still safe.

Frue went back to rebuild the breakwall yet again, this
time enlarging it to rise 18 feet above the lake, with a base
that extended 75 feet.

Winter came. Because the men had spent so much time
fighting the lake, they had only been able to build a log
cabin on the mainland, often by the light of lanterns after
they finished their shift on the rock. Some of the miners and
their families, who had come late that fall by boat, lived in
the single structure, but others spent the winter in tents.

It was a harsh time—even the log cabin had its problems.
Built hastily of green logs, the timbering shrank to let in
cold and hoarfrost. Food ran short; as the long, dark days
stretched on, the families had to chop holes in the ice to fish.
Nonetheless, the hardy community passed the first winter
without a single casualty. By spring, when the first boat arrived, Captain Frue had carried out over a million dollars
in silver ore—in 1870s prices.

More men and material were brought by boat to the wilderness. The area boomed. In only two years, the shoreline
boasted a church (complete with a widow's walk around its
steeple), schoolhouse, store, post office, and housing for five
hundred men. The officers of the company lived here, and
the silver community became known for its lavish hospi-
tality and its society. They had their own yacht, the *Silver
Spray,* and the stock of the company, when it could be
bought, went from $50 to $25,000 per share. Once again,
bold men had wrested a fortune out of the north country.

The islet expanded to ten times its original size ; despite
stormy seas, it had endured, though with continual repairs.
Its cribs, now greatly enlarged, conformed to the contours
of the lake bottom, filled with rock brought from the mainland by pickax, shovel, and wheelbarrow. On the rock-filled
top now were four boardinghouses, blacksmith and carpenter shops, offices, and the all-important boiler rooms.

As the mine went deeper, a shaft cut through a flaw in the lake's floor, and water began to pour through. In a desperate battle, the miners shored up the crack as best they could and brought in heavier water pumps. Though the pumps held back the water level, they knew all the same that Superior had begun the battle in earnest.

Storms add their own complications. Slamming out of the southeast, one December gale battered the fortress and carried away 350 feet of cribbing, 20,000 feet of timber, and tons of bolts, as well as huge rocks. It had broached the main breakwater, completely tearing away a building. Superior had picked up great rocks and tossed them about like hailstones.

Years passed. Below the surface, the mine had reached a depth of 1,230 feet, with 15 levels intersected by a main shaft, each 200 feet or more in length. As miners chased the main lode, it became elusive, sometimes narrowing down, then widening, in an increasingly expensive operation. Huge pumps ran continuously, noisily thumping out 155 gallons of water a minute. The islet was now dependent upon its manmade power run by coal brought in by steamers.

In 1884, the mine came to an end. The exact cause is shrouded in controversy. One story has it that Silver Islet's winter supply of coal, scheduled to arrive in November just prior to freeze-up, lay on board a steamer back in Houghton, Michigan. A drunken captain had let the vessel become frozen in. Over the winter months, the men on the isle had desperately fed their failing boilers every piece of wood they could collect from nearby forests. By March, coal and wood ran out and they began tearing wood from building walls. Slowly, deep below them in the mine, the lake gained. Soon the fires went out and the pumps stopped. In the icy silence, Superior had reclaimed its own.

That was the one version. Another, perhaps more realistic, was that the silver had thinned out. To pursue it further, the miners would have to dig upward toward the lake's surface, a dangerous procedure. Adding to these problems, in 1884 the price of silver had dropped. Some say the mine had just become too expensive to operate, and though, in fact, the shipload of coal had failed to arrive, it was just too late anyway for the mine to pay its way. Economics, not Superior, had finally closed the mine.

"Is the mine still out there?" I asked.

Ann smiled. "I've been out there many times. You can see the old shaft and some of the cribbing if you go over in a boat."

"Did you find any nuggets?"

"Oh, sure, we gathered some nuggets," she said, then showed me some of the fabulous silver. "This is what it looks like when you pull it up. This has pink dolomite in it, which is one of the characteristics of the silver here."

"And the shiny stuff—is that the silver?"

"That's the lead," Ann said. "The dark gray is silver."

The rocks I saw were laden with the dark silver, yet if I had not known what to look for, I would never have found it.

Still, the mine was so rich in native silver, I wondered whether anyone had ever tried to reopen it.

"In 1920, they tried, but they didn't get down anywhere near the level of the original miners. It wasn't profitable and that was the end of it."

"Is there still silver down there?"

"Oh, yes. Nobody knows how much. They say that when the original miners got down so far, they carved pillars and the roofs out of almost solid silver. But if you take the roof or a pillar out, you are doomed."

Ann continued: "I talked with skin divers, quite some time ago—they're not allowed down there, you know—but they were there anyway, taking pictures. They saw picks and shovels just sticking out of the walls where the miners had hurriedly left them, but they couldn't touch them or anything else for fear of bringing it all down on them."

In the long rays of the setting sun, I walked up the winding old avenue. I could see on the horizon, about a mile offshore, a large, dark-colored rock, barely above the waters of Superior. Its smooth surface did indeed remind me of a human skull. A few gnarled bushes clung tenaciously to the dark surface.

I knew without question what I was looking at. Still, it was hard for me to believe that for fourteen years this had been the world's greatest silver mine.

The map shows:
NORTH · PORT ARTHUR · THUNDER BAY · WELCOME ISLANDS · GRAND REEF · CANADA · PIE ISLAND · DEADMAN ISLAND · MINK ISLAND · SPAR ISLAND · VICTORIA ISLAND · CLOUD ISLANDS · BORDER · GRAND PORTAGE · SUSIE ISLANDS · LAKE SUPERIOR · VOYAGE OF PERSISTENCE - - - - - - - - -

15

PASSAGE TO THUNDER BAY

I COULD FEEL THE CRISPNESS IN THE AIR AND COULD SEE the foliage turning yellow and red. Fall was beginning to arrive, and with it, the most dangerous period for storms.

But as I studied Superior, it seemed to me that the big sea was calming itself, for a short time at least.

This would be one last opportunity for me to get in the water. I had been off the lake long enough, and though the time seemed longer, I had been exploring the north shore by automobile only about a week.

I made my decision: Time to complete my voyage north.

My family also had reached a decision.

"We're coming with you!" they said.

At first, I worried. But then I thought hard about our chances. The storm seemed to have blown itself out; the water, though choppy, did not look especially dangerous. Also, I knew we would only have a few hours on the open waters, then we'd be in the relatively protected waters of the big bay, under the shadow of the Sleeping Giant. I would be taking the island passageway route into Canada: along the north shore, past the Susie Islands, across the border, then, ducking into Thunder Bay—some of the most spectacular scenery on the lake.

They'd never get to see anything like this, except by boat. Perhaps they *should* join me on this final leg of my voyage to Canada.

"Let's do it!" I agreed. And so we took my car up to the Gunflint Trail, where *Persistence* rested on her trailer, and launched her at a small dock near Grand Portage.

As we rigged our sailboat, one woman stopped by to tell us how their large powerboat had been caught in heavy waves—their motor swamped.

"For a while, waves were practically breaking on board," the woman said, her face draining white, "and we were thinking of calling for help." But she said they got their engine started again to finally make port.

She had looked at our little sailboat, and blurted out, "You're not going out." Then, suddenly realizing we were, she walked away, muttering, "The *whole* family."

At six o'clock the next morning, the lake was already restless and I knew there would be worse to come. Still, I had a plan. We would get an early start, duck inside the island chain, and be off the lake before the big sea started kicking up.

It would be a race to the protection of the islands, and a rough one at that. I wanted to be certain of my wife's resolve. She sat in the cockpit opposite me, huddling down in her parka.

"We can still turn back," I said.

"No!" she replied. "I want to sail to Thunder Bay!"

We sailed out of the headlands guarding Grand Portage, entering the big sea. Beyond the Susie Islands, on the shore, I could see the Sawtooth Mountains rise straight up from the surf below. Waves slammed into an outer reef, curling white water upward in a spectacular shower—dangerous, too.

"Isn't that beautiful?" Loris asked, enjoying her passage.

"Certainly is," I said. I did not share her sense of esthetics right then, and gave us a little more sea room in case of reefs. From the quarter berth below came Bill's soft snores.

I had timed our adventure almost perfectly. As we approached the inland passage area, the lake awoke with a great scream from the northwest.

We had only a few miles of open water left before we were into the inner passage leading to Thunder Bay. Ahead, pine-covered islands jutted out of the blue waters.

We were running true north. My arm felt strong and my grip was powerful on the tiller.

"The boat is handling just fine," Loris said. I nodded in agreement.

I realized that we had long since slipped over the border into Canadian waters. Off to my starboard, white water curled straight up reefs, booming up on a sheer rock cliff.

Then we ducked behind an island and the whole day changed to bright and mild; the waters calmed. We had begun our passage inward to Thunder Bay.

"This is very historic. The ancient Voyageurs used the passage also," I said. "Some of their original camps were on these islands."

"Probably nothing has changed," Loris said, looking at the wilderness.

"Maybe I should wake Bill."

"Why don't you just let him sleep a bit longer?"

I pointed the bow to a small channel, and the boat seemed to squirt through to follow Mink Island. But it began to roll a bit as we entered the open waters of the bay.

"What's ahead?" I asked, seeing Loris had the charts. The wind had picked up again and so had the waves. We had left the temporary protection of the island chain.

"Deadman Island," Loris called back. I frowned as I pulled out my binoculars to scan ahead. It was alive with white plumes of water smashing into reefs. We were now heading directly for them, roaring along downwind. I was fighting for sea room. In this wind, *Persistence* was making leeway, and if we got shoved further, we'd be right on the reefs.

"The water's getting shallow in here," Loris said.

She hauled out two charts of Thunder Bay, a Canadian and an American. One showed enough depth for us to squeeze past Deadman to go around a nearby island. The other didn't.

"We're out of sea room," I hollered. "I can't pinch her any tighter to the reefs. We're going in!"

My grip tightened on the tiller; Loris became white-faced as we slid around the reef-strewn area. I half expected the bottom to hit at any moment. But then we were past—Loris and I turned to each other with relief.

Our next course took us past Grand Reef, toward the Welcome Islands. I was amazed at the quickness of the water and how the the waves could build so steep and sharp. It seemed as though one moment we were down in them, surrounded by water, then suddenly, we were in the air and able to see miles in any direction.

I was steering carefully so we didn't get caught the wrong way in the waves. Occasionally, *Persistence* would roar down one green comber to bury her bow in the back of the next. Green water would come rushing over the deck.

We moved as far forward in the cockpit as we could get, huddling against the cabin. This gave the boat a little more buoyancy in the stern. Now she could lift quicker to the onrushing graybeards that slammed into her transom.

"Reefs!" Loris yelled.

I looked about, desperately. "I can't see them."

"On the charts," she said, "they should be around here somewhere. The area is littered with them."

"I see one!" Loris said, her voice tight. "Over there!"

I strained my eyes, and then I saw a pole with a small flag atop it—the sure warning of a reef below.

"And over there!"

I altered course.

Now we were getting a great pounding, *Persistence* surfing forward, bow down into the trough, wildly pitching.

A sudden thought came to me. "How's Bill doing?"

Between lurches of the boat, Loris peered into the cabin. "He's reading."

"I don't believe it," I said. Still clutching my tiller, I leaned forward. There was my son, in his sleeping bag, reading a book. The boat shuddered, I corrected, and I could see green water against the portlight directly beside his head.

"How're you doing?" I asked.

"Fine."

"We're having quite an adventure out here. Want to take a look?"

"No, thanks."

"Can you see anything?"

"Yeah. I looked out a couple of times."

"Mind putting on a life preserver?"

"Aw, Dad! Do I have to?"

It seemed to be a terrible imposition, but he agreed. Grumbling, he put down his book, peeled himself out of the warm sleeping bag, and put on the life preserver. He gave me a rueful glance, then snuggled back into his sleeping bag to resume reading.

I was about to say something more, but I realized that he'd be as safe there as out with us in the cockpit.

We flew toward the Welcome Islands. I saw a large keelboat come out of the island's lee, catch the wind, put her beam down in a near capsize, right herself, then sail off.

"Someone's out with us!" I was overjoyed. Loris managed a wan smile, but her expression indicated she wondered what I was so happy about. Our situation was growing worse.

We were past the Welcome Islands, roaring toward the shore. We needed to find the entryway in the breakwater or else we'd go up on the rocks. It had to be around here somewhere.

"See anything?" I asked, growing nervous.

"No," Loris said. She was scanning the horizon with binoculars as we went aloft on a wave crest. "I can see grain terminals and even boxcars. But nothing else."

I took the binoculars with one hand. I could see a thin white line straight ahead. Surf pounding over something! The breakwall!

"We're coming in hard," I said, "and we don't have much maneuvering room in this wind. We've *got* to know where the entryway is. Try the VHF."

It was a desperate move. During this voyage, I had never been successful with a radio call to a marina.

"Thunder Bay marina . . . Thunder Bay marina . . . this is *Persistence*. Over," Loris called. Once, twice.

A crackle on the radio. "Thunder Bay marina to *Persistence*," a deep voice boomed in return.

"I've raised them," Loris said.

"See if you can find out where we are. We seem to be headed right toward a pink grain elevator."

"You're too far north," the voice drawled in answer. "Head more westerly. Look for a flashing light. That's the lighthouse marking the entryway."

"Thank you!" Loris said. She turned toward me with a happy grin.

I adjusted my heading, taking a whalloping from the wave trains. Minutes later, Loris shouted: "I've got it! There!"

She pointed her arm and then I saw the tiny blinking green light. The lighthouse.

"Almost got it made, pal!" I said.

"Not quite," Loris cautioned.

From behind the north breakwall, I saw a large ship emerge—about to cross the entryway directly in our path.

I watched as an onrushing wave struck the emerging ship; it caught the boat broadside, then seemed to climb right up to the top, and over. The boat was buried in white water. "A tour ship," I said, amazed. I saw some surprised passengers peering out from behind the portlights. Then, with a spurt of power, it was safe behind the other wall.

Suddenly, we were past the lighthouse and into the sheltered channel. The wind became mild, the water turned blue and calm; above us, the sun shone warmly. We were surrounded by sail boarders.

The harbormaster's boat approached, and I saw him motion for us to follow. We sailed past the sail boarders, then entered yet another breakwall of huge boulders to tie up at a dock.

Dave York, the marina supervisor, looked down at us. "You sure surprised me," he said. "I just happened to be in the office when I heard your call.

"And I sure never expected to see a boat this size out in those waves today," he said, shaking his head.

We had arrived.

16

END
OF THE
VOYAGE

HIGH WINDS WHIPPED THE MARCHING GRAY SOLDIERS OF the lake, making them rise and fall in unison, then crash upon the waiting rocks. There was chill in the air. No doubt about it, the great white north was fast freshening into fall.

In the protection of the harbor, I felt the sun's feeble glow on my face and its warmth in my snug cockpit. We bobbed in our safe berth, *Persistence* tugging at her lines, but it was all over. My family had returned home. Though the boat was ready for more passage making, I was not. I waited.

People stopped by to talk and tell me news. Another singlehander had disappeared, up on the Canadian north shore. He was the second solo sailor who had vanished on the big lake during my voyage. One at the beginning—and now another.

The lost sailor was a veteran who knew the lake in all its moods and who had sailed long distances alone in his wooden boat. One day, his white sloop had been found shipwrecked on the rocks near Silver Islet, sails still set. The tragedy had a profound effect on me.

She bobbed gently by a grassy embankment near the far pier, her tall wooden masts projecting into the sky, sails laced to her booms. It was the *Carioca*; I had heard about her and the singlehander who sailed her. Some said he was a dreamer, like me, a man who built wooden boats the old way and sailed them alone on Superior's cold waters.

With his white beard and dark clothing, he was well known to the waterfront community—a sort of perpetual wanderer upon the lake. With fall in the air, he had returned.

His name was Albert Leon. To me, he was a national treasure. The grizzled old shipwright knew the traditional ways of building; he had constructed by hand from ancient plans replicas of some of the first boats upon this lake.

Now he was seated in the cockpit of his old sloop, looking off into the distant horizon. Perhaps he saw something I did not; perhaps he heard something I couldn't hear. I began to introduce myself, but he already knew who I was.

The old shipwright invited me on board. He had hit a reef out there, but did not seem concerned that the *Carioca* was slowly sinking.

"Do you want a beer?" he politely offered. I accepted, and we settled down in the cockpit to talk of other times on the lake, just as if it were the most natural thing in the world to do.

When he was off Superior, the shipwright demonstrated boatbuilding at Old Fort William. Dressed in traditional shipwright's gear, he worked with native woods, slowly carving his creations with ancient tools. Old Fort William's wooden stockade and buildings stood at Pointe de Meuron, along a Voyageur route up the Kaministikwia River from Lake Superior. Explorers and trappers had paddled and portaged on this "fur highway" as far north as the Arctic ice and as far west as the Pacific.

It was at Old Fort William that the old shipwright had built his boats and had created his masterpiece, a large

wooden schooner built the old way, plank by plank, of lo-
cally grown white pine, spruce, birch, ash, elm, and tamarack. Crooks of tamarack or pine had served as ribs;
woodsmen with half-inch pine patterns were sent into the
bush to search for naturally grown wood that matched. The
boat had taken him many years—he wasn't finished yet.
That this was his seventh summer and his boat's name was
Perseverance gave me pause: it had taken me seven years,
and my boat's name was *Persistence*. An odd coincidence.

The schooner was a majestic-looking craft—I had seen it
at the fort—with tall masts raking the heavens, a hull
length of 60 feet, a beam of 17 feet, and a draft of 7 feet.
The boat looked fit to carry its 70-ton capacity of cargo anywhere on the Great Lakes.

To build his big ship, the old shipwright had researched
original documents for old sailing vessels, including an
1812 warship that the Royal Navy had used in a battle on
Lake Huron. The most difficult part of using old techniques
had been steaming the wood to make the curves. In the old
days, he said, the curves up front were so tight that just one
knot in a plank could make it break.

I was amazed he could build so large a craft with only
hand tools, and wondered if they were as good as modern
power tools. "When you get the hang of them, they are," the
old shipwright said. "The adz, for example, is very efficient.
I got so I did everything with it, including sharpening my
pencil. You can cut curves, cut straight, reduce a board by a
sixteenth of an inch, or take off an inch at a whack. It's my
favorite tool, and I've still got both legs."

"What?"

"I've got both legs because I've avoided using the
broadax. The head of it weighs about three times as much as
an adz, and your leg has to be on the same side you're chop-
ping. With an adz, you have to straddle a log, and if the
head slips, it just slips between your legs. I've found that
with a chalk line and an adz, I can make a round pole, or
taper it. We even made our masts that way."

"How old are your actual working tools?" I asked.

"Anywhere from eighty to a hundred and fifty years old," he responded happily. "On some of them, the hand-grip is so small I can only get two fingers in them."

"Why is that?"

"Smaller men. I've got one four-foot jackplane with a hole in it, not a handle, and when I use it, one of my fingers just sticks out. The plane must have weighed nearly as much as the man using it."

I had always imagined the men who braved the wilderness were hearty giants of the north woods. He shook his head, then told me that the original Voyageurs who came here were only a little over five feet tall.

"*That* short?" I could not conceal my amazement.

"Yes, but they were muscular," he continued. "They had to be, for their work would either make a person muscular or dead. But I believe they were stronger than we are. Think of the Voyageurs carrying two and three ninety-pound packs on the Grand Portage. It was nine miles uphill over a very rocky trail."

"But why did they carry so much?"

"They had a choice: Each Voyageur was obliged to carry so many packs up the trail, so they could either carry one pack and make two or three trips, or carry all the packs at once, then rest. So a lot of Voyageurs carried three packs, each weighing ninety pounds."

He paused. "If you can get anyone these days, even six feet tall, to carry a ninety-pound pack up that portage, they probably wouldn't speak for weeks—they'd be in a state of total collapse."

I was curious about the Voyageur's birchbark canoe. It was a legend—a beautifully shaped basket of cedar, spruce, and birchbark, ultralightweight for carrying through the woods, yet strong enough for men to use it to brave Superior.

The old shipwright told me the fort built two or three of them each season, and smiled as he said, "We never had a birchbark canoe that didn't leak badly. They leaked in those days, too.

"The Indian used to load his canoe properly, which is to say very little. But the Voyageurs regularly overloaded them, putting two-and-a-half tons in a twenty-six-footer, four tons in a thirty-six-footer. Birch was never designed by nature for anything that heavy.

"In winter, they used to sink the canoes in rivers so that they would not dry out," he continued. "They'd fill them full of rocks, and sink them under water, and when they'd take them out, they were just like when they were put in. If you hung them up on stands, from fall to spring, all the cedar lining and ribs would shrink; that would make the birchbark loose, and the ribs would just fall out of the boat, since there's nothing holding them in. They are not tied or sewed, just tucked in. It's the water that was always leaking in that kept the canoes tight."

"How well did the bigger birchbark canoes handle?"

"The steering was done from the bow, and the helmsman was an expert. As a matter of fact, he was paid almost twice as much as the standard paddler. That's because if he made a mistake, good-bye canoe and probably most of the crew, since few of them could swim. But with a full load, canoes don't turn well at all. You get the feeling you're on a hand-car, and you're trying to turn, but the canoe wants to stay on the track and go straight ahead."

"It's amazing how well the Voyageurs did with what they had," I said. "But what strikes you the most about them, from all you've learned?"

He thought only for a moment, this six-footer of a ship-builder. "I never get over the amazement of how strong they were," he said.

"What else?"

"They came from the farm. Think about it: in spring, they planted their crop, and they had very little to do till harvest. So they signed on with a company to go a couple thousand miles into the wilderness. They were absolutely at the mercy of their employers, though, and the work was terribly hard and dangerous. Some of them came back home with hernias and ruptures, which made them totally useless."

"How did farmers get to be so good with canoes?" I asked.

"You have to remember that farms originally were scattered up the Saint Lawrence River," he said. "No farming was done inland since there were no roads."

"How long did they stay Voyageurs?"

"Records show that only one in seven signed up for a second year. Think about that. One in seven."

So we sat, talking, on the slowly sinking sailboat. From time to time, he checked the bilge, and once, so did I. Indeed, the creeping water was visible; the sight of it gave me a shudder. But I did not want to get off the boat.

The old shipwright's schooner had hit a reef on an island in Amethyst Harbour. "I thought I had run out of luck," he said. "I hit hard, but luckily, a couple of large waves came along and boosted the whole boat—bouncing me from one rock to another—and finally just shoved me off."

I shook my head. This old boat had bounced sideways across the reefs in the high winds and seas; he had emerged shaken and with a badly leaking boat. But still afloat.

I could not see the leak and neither could he. He had surmised, though, that it was underneath some planking.

"Not surprising, considering the sudden shocks that had pushed the frames upward," he said. Then he shrugged and added, "The damage may swell up or realign itself." He had faith.

I leaned back in the cockpit, feeling the sun on my shoulders and the gentle fall wind on my face. I thought I saw something distant in the mists of the horizon beyond the harbor. This was where the old shipwright had been looking, too. There was something shining, white—maybe a sail-boat—and then it was gone. I was not even certain I had seen it.

A scene in the movie *Jeremiah Johnson* flashed through my mind. Two mountain men sit high above the snowline, looking out into the distance. They had been in the mountains a long time; one of them—I think it was Robert Redford—asks what season of the year it was—as casually as if he had asked for the time.

"Sorry, Pilgrim," the other man answers. He guesses it might be April, maybe May, but he does not really care. And so they sit staring out at nothing in particular, waiting, lost like pilgrims in a world they had been caught up in.

And so it was now for me.

The boat might sink, it might not. I finished my beer and was about to leave, when I turned to ask him if there was anything I could do since I was berthed where I could see his boat. He seemed to look out at the horizon, then finally shrugged his shoulders.

"Take a bearing from time to time on my masts and the stars," he said. "And if my masts aren't up there, you know I am in trouble."

"Sure enough," I agreed.

As I walked away, I thought I heard the word, "Pilgrim," uttered softly, somewhere.

17

DREAMS
OF DISTANT
SHORES

STREAMS OF FREEWAY TRAFFIC SURGED AROUND MY speeding car. It was a winter day with no shadows; in the distance, beyond the freeway ring, loomed the landscape of the city, not yet covered with the mercy of snow. Tall slabs of apartment buildings jutted upward here and there on the hills. I felt faintly depressed even though I looked forward to a noontime meeting with the Old Commodore of Madeline Island. It would be in the Summit Hill area of old St. Paul.

Only a few months had passed since I winched my boat from Superior's waters. As I headed south, out of Canada and down the north shore, the world had been transformed; summer had slowly returned. The autumn-hued trees had given way to green foliage.

I slowed down as I turned into my own neighborhood and approached my house on Brigadoon Drive, to savor my homecoming. This was where I had created *Persistence* and the neighbors had watched her take shape and shared my dream. I could see the smoke of backyard barbecues and imagined my neighbors on their patios enjoying one of the last days of summer. I felt sad, though, that no one was around in the fading light to welcome me or my boat back from our great adventure.

For weeks the boat sat awkward and abandoned atop her trailer in our cement driveway. All the scars of our northward battles were visible on her hull—I did not have the energy to epoxy her scars, redo her varnish, and to repaint her torn waterline. But I knew that under all she was still sound and a very strong little boat. All she would need was to have some time spent on her.

I needed time, too. I had changed and not just physically. True, my face was as deeply tanned as any Voyageur's, although there were rings around my eyes where my eyeglass frames had screened out the sun. My hair was unruly, curly and wild, as well as much too long. I had lost over 15 pounds; my body felt gaunt inside my clothing.

I was tired and lethargic. Nature was making me slow down and restore myself. I would spend long periods of time in our backyard, soaking up the warmth of the sun, trying to overcome the stiffness and soreness. But most of all, I was trying to reorient myself to the world again. My mind seemed far away.

One day the Old Commodore called; he was delighted to hear of my safe return. He confessed he had been worried about me and *Persistence*. Would I meet him for lunch at a small restaurant in town?

Now, when I saw him again, I began to feel better. He was still the hearty veteran I remembered, talking and joking, recalling anecdotes of his sailing days on the big lake. He listened with interest to my tales of waves and winds, of the everlasting fog, of the northeaster I'd found on the north shore. He told me he knew of them, too, and smiled his old sea dog smile.

A chart of the lake was embedded in his memory—he recalled names of places, directions, and locations with ease. He told me of parts of Superior that I had not yet seen, of shimmering, green islands on the horizon, of radiant, clear harbors, of north woods and still waters that few had known since the days of the Voyageurs.

A dream lived on in his mind that he was trying to share with me—a special feeling for places he had been and coastlines, islands, and open waters he had once seen. As I listened, I felt that Superior had marked and changed him, as my three months on the lake had changed me. I realized I couldn't escape it—Superior was reaching out toward me and was beckoning. I knew that someday soon I would return.

18

EPILOGUE

LAKE SUPERIOR TODAY IS AS BROAD AND VAST AS ever—a technicolor lake of dreams. At times, it still catches the unwary.

The summer of 1984, when I took my voyage on my little centerboard sloop, *Persistence,* I ran afoul of bad weather. In 1988, when the hard-cover edition of this book came out, sailors on the ever-changeable lake enjoyed some of its best weather—one of the finest summers in recent memories, as one mariner told me. Some sailors, who were new to the Big Lake, wondered what I was writing about.

The next year, they found out. The Coast Guard's 180-foot cutter *Mesquite* was lost on a shoal off the tip of Keeweenaw Point. Though all 53 crew members were rescued, storms with 18-foot seas and 50 mile-per-hour winds damaged the steel ship beyond repair. She now lies beneath Superior's cold waters.

Over the years since I took my voyage, the Big Lake's people have changed. Rufus Jefferson (p.43), the legendary sailor of the lake, is now missing at sea. At about 4:30 p.m., on September 23, 1990, he sailed out from his home on Madeline Island in a small boat of his own design—and simply disappeared. Despite extensive air and sea searches, neither his body, his gear, nor his boat have ever been recovered.

The Red Baron (p.38) still enjoys flying. When I was first up on the lake, the young flyer took his pup up in his aircraft, wedging him between his legs. But soon Wolf no longer could accompany the Red Baron on his flights throughout the 600-square-mile Apostle Island Group. "He just got too big," he explained to me, "although he enjoyed it hugely." The part-wolf dog (p.39) came to weigh nearly 100 pounds.

His ultra-light, *Beauford T.*, also has changed. "I was out flying one day," he explained, "and the motor quit." In the heavily wooded islands, there are few landing places, even for the Baron. Huge pines stuck up to the skies; in between trees and brush struggled in an ancient battle for sunlight. "So I picked a nice big pine," he continued, nonchalantly, "and landed in it. The tip and the branches accepted the impact just fine. I stopped about 100 feet from the ground, and then we fell down the branches. I wasn't hurt." Now he has a new aircraft, which is an exact duplicate of his original *Beauford T*, complete with identical 55-h.p. engine. On a sad note, Wolf was caught and died in a baited trap on Madeline Island.

Today fewer people remain year-around on Madeline, including the Baron, who now lives atop a bluff near Bayfield, where he can look over most of the islands. Life on an island has its difficulties and hardships During the winter of 1992-93, the ice road (p.34) that connects the island with the mainland did not freeze over until mid-February and the only transportation was the islander's unique ice sled. That sled (p.36) runs through the water and ice floes every day, though the World War II Army surplus M-4 tank engine had been replaced by a 450-cubic inch Chevrolet engine, now spinning twin propellers.

The Old Digger of the Islands, Al Galazen (p.28), died in 1992. The islanders held a memorial at the Island's museum, where he had contributed so many of the historical artifacts that he dug up on the island. I recall one time when I was on the island spending an evening with him and Wayne Nelson (alias the Red Baron) in his small wooden house beside the shores of the lake. He told us many tales of his digging and his discoveries. He was a wonderful man and he will be missed.

Up and down the shores of the Big Lake, many other changes have occurred. In Cornucopia, the folksy little bar (p.65) that I discovered one hot day has changed ownership. Correspondents sadly report that the bar's usual charge of 25 cents a glass beer (p.66) is history. The Cornucopia Yacht Club's (p.76) founding father and guiding light, Roger O'Malley, passed away. Maybe some day we'll meet O'Malley on the yacht club's fabled Pier 99 (p. 78).

Capt. Jim Frostman (p. 70), still fishes, though life for a commercial fisherman on Lake Superior is very difficult these days, with many restrictions.

But near the water's edge, as you head down Hwy. 13, the Good Earth still stands. Here Curtis and Ruth Johnson (p.66), meet travelers along the road much as they did when I sailed my boat into Cornucopia. They are wonderful people and I look forward to visiting them when I am up on the lake.

To me, Lake Superior is full of adventures—and you can never tell when the next one will arise. One summer day, the Johnsons invited me to Cornucopia to sign copies of my book and to do my slide show, *Shipwrecks and Old Salts of the Shining Big Sea*. After my presentation, an elderly sports fisherman came up, somewhat apologetically, and began a story that amazed me.

"I don't know what you want to do with this, but we saw something out there," he said, explaining that he and his wife had been in their boat on their way back to the Cornucopia harbor when they noticed something odd in their electronic "fishfinder." "We were on a line with it," he explained. "First we saw the stern section and the cabin come into view. Then we were over the long spar deck. And then we clearly saw what looked like the pilot house, with its mast sticking up in the water."

"Did you get a bearing on shore?" I asked, astounded.

"No, we were too busy looking at the wreck. But she lines up between Bark Point in 100 feet of water. If you go straight out from the entry until you hit that depth, you should be in a line between the two points. And that's where you'll find her."

A shipwreck? A call to the experts at the Marine Museum in Duluth told me that no, there were no known large shipwrecks in that harbor—too far off the shipping lanes. True, there was an old tug sunk years ago near the entryway, but nothing like the vessel estimated by the fisherman to be between 300 and 350 feet in length.

I went out with a party of divers in their Zodiac, equipped with Loran and depthsounder. For hours, the Zodiac lazed along at about three knots, engine turning over at little better than trolling speed. I watched the picture being drawn of what was below us at about 100 feet. In between, I saw black dots. Many large black dots.

"Just fish." The divers seemed uninterested.

By mid-afternoon, we had done our full Loran search, plus a generous overlap area. Nothing.

The September day had been unusually hot on Superior, but I wondered at the mugginess. I was perspiring heavily, but looked up to notice a strange darkening of the waters. Within minutes, the wind had switched to a northeasterly direction, and, with a gust, shook the open boat. The waves started sending spray into the boat. We had encountered a storm, and minutes later, something else.

"What's that?" I saw a block-like appearance on the bottom of the depthsounder graph. It seemed to rise out of the bottom below us. "Very interesting," the diver said, immediately turning the boat. "Now comes the high-tech part," he said with a wry grin, tossing a heavy anchor tied to a nylon line into the water. Then he wrapped the end of the rope around his shoulder.

I must have looked puzzled, so he explained: "I can feel it skipping off the bottom, just barely digging in at times," he said. He was dragging the anchor over the bottom to "feel" what it might snag. Presumably, if the anchor caught, there was something down there—and I hoped he would stay in the boat when it did.

We scoured the area with depthsounder and anchor. Then the diver brought up the anchor, hand over hand. The expedition was over, but the questions remained.

"What could the fisherman have seen?" I asked.

The divers shook their heads. Whatever it was, it wasn't

there when we searched. And I had double-checked: we had the right bearings and depth.

"Actually, this is one of the better reports we've gotten," the diver said. "Sometimes people think they see things down in the water or hear of old rumors of wrecks. Here we had a specific report on an LCD, with specific bearings and even a depth. And whatever was supposed to be down there then, isn't there now."

The waves slapped the sides of the Zodiac as he lifted off the underwater gear. Then we headed back toward the entryway, with the engine now at a healthy snarl. We began to plane over the water, catching the speeding waves and surfing down their fronts. It was a wild, exhilarating ride, and all too soon we were inside the entryway, and in the calm waters of the small harbor.

The lead diver shook his head sadly. It had been a careful search, but it had yielded no results. A lost ship of Superior had eluded us, despite a promising lead. "In many ways, to look for lost ships, you really have to believe in Santa Claus," he concluded as he let the air out of the inflatable.

But I knew these, and other divers would be back. Somewhere in the depths of this, the deepest, largest and coldest of the Great Lakes, were still a number of "lost" vessels, just waiting to be discovered. Some of these are well-preserved in Superior's cold waters—a storehouse of history for the lucky diver.

Over the years, particularly with the advent of the "fish-finder", a number of new shipwrecks have been found. I have often wondered about how many boats there actually are on Superior's chill depths. Historical and other published articles offer a wide diversity of estimates and figures. I turned for advice to several shipwreck experts.

C. Patrick Labadie, of the Canal Park Marine Museum in Duluth, pointed out some of the difficulties of arriving at a comprehensive survey because records were inexact on shipwrecks, particularly before the turn of the century. He said that not all vessels and casualty occurrences have been reported around the lake. Small or unregistered vessels simply may not have been included in the total. But so far as documentation is concerned, Pat told me, "there have been 350 total losses of ships on Lake Superior, and 7,000 to 8,000 on the Great Lakes overall." He added, "I suspect as many as 10,000 if relatively small vessels are included (like tugs.)"

Thom Holden (p.123), now assistant curator of the Marine Museum, broke down the shipwreck figures this way: the 350 shipwrecks documented were total losses, without salvage, and now lie beneath the lake's surface. He estimated that to the figure of total loss shipwrecks could be added another 1,500 to 2,000 major accidents, where something significant happened to the boat, or someone was killed, but that the accidents resulted in repair or refloating of the vessels, and not their abandonment. To these figures of shipwrecks of all kinds, he estimated, there could be added another 1,500 to 2,000 lesser accidents or mishaps. The figures represent large, commercial vessels, with a few small undocumented boats included.

One of the greatest of Superior's shipwrecks, The *Edmund Fitzgerald* (p.116), celebrated in song and in legend as the *Titanic* of Superior, still remains shrouded in mystery. She sank Nov. 10, 1975, so quickly that she did not even have time to cry out for help. Underwater surveys with unmanned submersibles were send down to her final resting place beneath 530 feet of Superior's chill waters. A recent dive with stereo-video equipment, which took a careful look at the pilot house, the forward cabins, and at the debris fields near the stern, captured new details but brought no further conclusions to solve the mystery.

Why did she sink? After the publication of the hardcover edition of this book, readers interested in the mystery got in touch with me. One reader sent me photographs of the *Fitzgerald* he had taken the summer before she sank. It showed, unmistakably, a great crease along her starboard aft section, as if she had rammed something. An expert I asked to look at the picture told me it suggested the hull was weakened. More evidence also came out that the crew was concerned about repairs made on the hull, years before, and that the big ship had a distinct "wiggle."

1 At about 15:20, the *Edmund Fitzgerald* hits a reef. The reef ruptures the hull and water pours in, causing a list, and hydraulic pressure blows off vents. She becomes a slowly sinking vessel.

2 At about 19:15, the *Fitzgerald* sudder plunges bow-first to the bottom 530 away, carrying all crew members with h Her end comes so quickly she did not h time to cry out for help. She remains int going down, but when the bow strikes, 729-foot vessel's cargo shifts and the hu breaks apart under the impact.

Fitzgerald

3 The 253-foot aft section turns over, lying bottom up. The 276-foot forward section sits upright, as if ready to sail on. In between lies a junkyard. All of the crew perished with her and lie entombed in the wreck.

Though all ore boats have some flexibility when they encounter heavy seas, the *Fitzgerald's* bow wandered so much that the Captain repeatedly had expressed concern when his boat began "that wiggling thing." That the *Fitzgerald* had taken a mauling prior to her sinking was apparent.

Several mariners told me about the voyage of a large vessel that set out the following summer after the *Fitzgerald* sank. On board were divers who were not interested in the final resting place of the *Fitzgerald*—that's far too deep for divers anyway—but rather upon a certain reef. Specifically, a *newly identified* reef in Six Fathom Shoals.

The official Coast Guard underwater investigation (p. 122) was only on the wreck itself. It began the following May when the Coast Guard Cutter *Woodrush* surveyed the wreck with a tethered, remotely operated underwater research vehicle known as an ROV. More dives were logged on the wreck, shooting 43,000 feet of videotape and taking nearly 900 color photographs. But, officially, no U.S. Coast Guard divers checked out the reef that might have torn the bottom of the big ore carrier.

The "new" reef at Six Fathom Shoal, unknown to the captain of the *Fitzgerald*, was officially identified only the following year when the Canadian Hydrographic Service made a new survey. The resulting data clearly showed a *newly identified reef* slightly more than one mile due east of previously identified reefs at position 47°26.8'N, 85° 47, 6'W. There are two depth soundings near it of 8 and 9 fathoms. The new reef is 5.2 fathoms in depth—shallow enough to have ruptured the bottom out of the*Fitzgerald* in storm conditions.

The *Fitzgerald* tragedy was the greatest loss financially in the history of Great Lakes sailing, worth nearly $24 million in replacement costs at the time she sank. That figure is for the ship only and does not include the cost of her cargo. The official findings basically held that the storm caused the giant carrier's fatal plunge—an accident due to an act of nature. Yet if it could have been proven that the *Fitzgerald* was off course and had hit a reef, the speculation is that lawsuits for untold millions could have been initiated, not only for the ship and cargo, but especially for the loss of the 28-man crew.

Reconstructing the tragic events, it is likely that the *Fitzgerald's* captain cut in too close to Six Fathom Shoal, north of Caribou Island. Capt. Jessie Cooper, on board the *Anderson* miles back which had the *Fitzgerald* on its radar, noted alarmingly that "he's in too close. He's closer than I'd want this ship to be."

On that raging lake that November afternoon, Captain McSorly saw nothing specifically indicated on charts to cause him to suspect the danger that lurked beneath the huge waves. There, on a shoal that was not identified on the charts, he smashed his vessel's bottom. Minutes later, he reported that he had taken on a list and had his pumps on—but even this was not enough to right the vessel, which had taken on a 15-degree list. As he sailed on, the *Fitzgerald* was a slowly sinking vessel losing freeboard (which accounts for his radio report, "it's the worst sea I've ever been in.") His vessel was boarded by huge waves. At about 7:15 p.m, a wave train struck and the *Fitzgerald* never recovered.

What happened? For more answers, I turned to the president of the Great Lakes Shipwreck Historical Society, Thomas L. Farnquist. The society has a superb museum at the tip of Whitefish Point, on the eastern end of Superior, not far from Sault Ste. Marie, Michigan. Here, near the Whitefish Point lightstation which entered service in 1849, a visitor can look out over the lake just about 17 miles to see where the *Fitzgerald* sank.

Farnquist told me he found it an "interesting point" that the Canadian government did not detect the reef earlier— before the *Fitzgerald* disaster. He said that he tends to agree with professionals who believe that the vessel sustained structural damage near Caribou Island. However, he felt that finding *where* the *Fitzgerald* may have touched bottom on the "new" reef may be difficult because of the vast amount of underwater area involved. "You'd have to run tight diving patterns to catch where the *Fitzgerald's* hull touched. You could go right by and not see it." He also told me that even a very well planned search would be "a difficult job at best" and that "it would be difficult to find evidence of hitting bottom."

What could have been identified on an early underwater survey, say, right after the big ore boat sank? "You could see scrape marks, gouges in the stone, some bottom paint, rust, and possibly metal scraps," he said, but added that now, years later, "would be a bad time since everything would be gone but the metal."

Could a metal detector pick up evidence of metal scrapings? He told me that in 35 feet of water, you'd have to go right over it to get a hit—within 100 feet. "Chances are that there is not much left," he said. I asked if he knew of any dive on the reef, and he told me of the work done by a Chicago professional: "Diver Dick Race contracted with his survey vessel, *Neptune*, to do a survey of the uncharted shoal off Caribou Island looking for evidence of a ship touching bottom. To my knowledge, nothing was found."

No accounts of the results of underwater searches by divers on the "new" reef were mentioned in the official U.S. Coast Guard Casualty Report on the accident, the Lake Carriers Association's response, nor in any of the published works about the mystery of the *Fitzgerald* that I had seen.

Today, as Farnquist points out, it may be much too late for amateur sleuthing.

But who knows what might be found, less than 30 feet down— so tantalizingly close?

I also was interested in the fate of the *L. L. Smith* (p. 90). I had tied up alongside this old tug during my voyage when it was a part of the Lake Superior Field Station, near the Superior entryway at the old Coast Guard station. She did wonderful work—taking school kids out on the lake to see how scientists studied Superior by sampling the water and bottom sediment. I had fond memories of this old vessel, so it was with surprise that, a few years later, I accompanied a concerned Mary Balcer to the Fraser Shipyards. There I saw the old tug propped up on shore, facing the uncertain prospects of being sold or salvaged because the Field Station had closed due to lack of funding. Now the *L.L. Smith* sails again as part of the University of Wisconsin-Superior's Lake Superior Research Institute. She offers workshops and programs and has three-hour school trips to take teachers and students out on the lake for an ecology cruise and to be "an aquatic scientist for three hours." I was out on one cruise and I recommend it. Dan Rau is now her captain and Mary Balcer is no longer the jeans-wearing marine biologist I met. Now she's *Doctor* Balcer.

Duluth (p. 86) has focussed its interests increasingly upon the lake. A splendid new Lakewalk has been built along the waterfront from the Aerial Lift Bridge over the Duluth ship entryway to Leif Erickson Park. The grassy little embankment where I tied up my little sailboat on my jaunts from Barker's Island (102) now has another vessel moored there, 610-foot *SS William A. Irvin*, a retired ore boat open for public tours. This is a fascinating vessel. Climb to the pilothouse and look over her vast decks. Then re-read the chapter on the sinking of the *Fitzgerald* (p.116) and try to imagine a dark, stormy day on the open waters of Superior when waves climb on board that long spar deck and roll forward to pile up behind the cabin in which you are standing. You gain some new appreciation for the skill and the courage of the sailors who ply this vast lake.

Not far away, the Lake Superior Center will help to focus new attention, interest and understanding on what has been referred to as "the last Great Lake."

Capt. Stanley Sievertson (p. 164) still is Captain of the *Wenonah*, but at age 79, he no longer goes out on every voyage. The *Wenonah* has changed to its voyage, too. Now the ship leaves the Grand Portage dock, in the shadows of the historic old fur fort, for a tour which includes a visit to the famed 100-year-old Witch Tree, the Susie Islands (p.191) and then across the open waters to Washington Harbor on Isle Royale (p.166). As a member of the historic fishing families on Isle Royale, Capt. Sievertson still takes time to do some commercial fishing and last year, he told me, he took out a skiff to catch nearly 600 trout.

Shipwright Albert Leon (p. 199 and picture pages) completed the large wooden schooner *Perseverance* at Old Fort William. With volunteers, he hand-built the replica 60-foot vessel based on original 1812 plans. I was on board the majestic schooner when it floated for several years in front of the old fur fort's stockade on the Kaministikwia River, near Thunder Bay. The Old Shipwright was dreaming of circumnavigating Superior in it—a beautiful voyage which would have brought a new sense of Great Lakes history to many people. Today, the schooner is gone, and I was told it had been sold to another historical center. The Old Shipwright no longer works at the fort, either.

Some people ask if I still have *Persistence*, the 20-foot centerboard sloop I built and sailed on Superior. My answer is that little wooden boats, like spouses and good friends, don't get older—they only get better. *Persistence* has been my constant companion every summer and usually has a berth on White Bear Lake, about 17 minutes from my home in Shoreview, Minnesota.

She has changed little since I took my voyage. I've added some electronic equipment, including a much-needed knot-meter and depth-sounder. A few years ago, I jacked her up and built a new stub keel for her, about six feet long and five inches deep. Now her centerboard pivots through the stub keel and so I technically have a keel-centerboard vessel. The stub keel adds about 50 percent more surface area to the keel area and gives me some much-needed ballast and makes her a lot more civilized to sail.

Persistence still shines bright in her all-varnish topsides, and there has to be a place in a lot of sailor's hearts for an all wooden boat like this, for people still come up to me and tell me how much they like her. Looking over the rows of fiberglass boats, one sailor gave me the "thumbs up" as he yelled over the water, "Now that's a real sailboat." As I said, she doesn't get older, she only gets better.

I have returned many times to the Big Lake, but not with my little vessel. Time and activity have closed in on me since when I was able to carve out a summer of voyaging. But I hope to return with *Persistence* one day.

The Big Sea has always called to me. It has a mystical quality that I never found anywhere else. Clambering upon its shores I have the feeling of destiny and of history.

Once I lived on its waters in my boat and was soothed by

its tranquility and shaken by its power. I heard its mournful foghorns on nights when no man should have been out in a small boat on its waters. I have been felt its fury in storms and in its waves.

It is a powerful place on this earth that it casts an aura on those who come near its mystical, cold waters. I can feel its presence not only on me but in my senses. And I have become addicted to it.

Superior is, to me, the last great lake. It is the largest body of water in the world that is still relatively unpolluted and still largely wild and free. Large segments of its 2,900-mile shoreline are still largely as wild and as untouched as when the first Voyageurs viewed them centuries ago. It is still very much a frontier of water and sky—perhaps a last frontier.

It is a magnet that draws me even as it uplifts and challenges me. It renews me when I return.

And I realize each time that I have been away too long.

—MARLIN BREE

ACKNOWLEDGMENTS

DURING MY VOYAGE, I WAS DEEPLY APPRECIATIVE OF THE people on Lake Superior's shores who opened a tugboat door, a guard shack, or a kitchen to me when I was in need of friendship and warmth. If Superior and the north country are at times wild and harsh, their natives are hospitable and kind—I never lacked for their support. I only hope that through this book I have done justice to this spirit of Superior.

I would also like to acknowledge my debt to those who shared with me their love of Superior and who provided their aid and assistance in developing this book. Some of its major insights come from the waterfront people. From them I was able to people the book—give it the flesh and blood of humanity.

I am also grateful to Gerry Spiess, of White Bear Lake, Minnesota, whose spirit of adventure is an inspiration to all who have small boats but dream of sailing big waters. He taught me that a proper voyage depends not upon the size of the boat but the stature of the sailor.

A number of people helped me make arrangements for my voyage. I am indebted to, in particular, Russell Fridley, former director of the Minnesota State Historical Society, and now director of the Margaret Chase Smith Library Center, and Donald G. Padilla, of Padilla, Speer, Burdick and Beardsley, and also president of the Charles A.

Lindbergh Fund. I am also indebted to the nautical wisdom of N. Bruce Roberts-Goodson, N.A. Though my boat saw the worst that Superior could throw at her during the storms I encountered, it sailed well—nothing broke. In addition, I want to thank John Ketzler, my amateur radio instructor, who taught me the ways of Morse code, leading to my novice license. I also appreciated the readings I received, on selected chapters, from Brian Richard Boylan, Minneapolis, and from Wayne Carpenter, Annapolis.

I am especially grateful for the expert literary counsel and editorial incisiveness of Clarkson N. Potter's staff, particularly of Jonathan Fox, with whom I worked closely on forging the initial drafts, as well as Executive Editor Nancy Novogrod, whose finely honed skills contributed so much to this book's final development. For bringing me to Clarkson N. Potter, I thank my literary representative, Mrs. Bobbe Siegel. She knows a classy outfit when she sees one.

Turning my dream into a reality would never have been possible without the loving support of my family, Loris and Bill. To them, I especially owe a debt of gratitude. I am aware of the loneliness and sometimes the pain I caused by my absence and by the adventures of my voyage. Yet I feel that the experience has been beneficial to us as a family and that we have grown closer and more loving from it.

Above all, I am grateful to whatever eternal powers there be that permitted me to bring back the story of this special world. As civilization closes upon me once again, I can only hope that something, somewhere, keeps Superior—the greatest lake—for all of us.

SELECTED
BIBLIOGRAPHY

Boyer, Dwight. *Ghost Ships of the Great Lakes.* New York: Dodd, Mead, 1984

———. *Great Stories of the Great Lakes.* New York: Dodd, Mead, 1966.

Bogue, Margaret Beattie, and Palmer, Virginia A. *Around the Shores of Lake Superior: A Guide to Historic Sites.* Madison, Wisc.: University of Wisconsin Sea Grant College Program, 1979.

Dahl, Bonnie. *The Superior Way: A Cruising Guide to Lake Superior.* Ashland, Wisc.: Inland Sea Press, 1983.

Engman, Elmer. *An Underwater Guide to the Western Half of Lake Superior.* Superior, Wisc.: Nordic Underwater Enterprises, 1974.

Havighurst, Walter. *The Long Ships Passing.* New York: Macmillan, 1975.

Hemming, Robert J. *Gales of November: The Sinking of the Edmund Fitzgerald.* Chicago: Contemporary Books, 1981.

Holden, Thom. *Above and Below: A History of Lighthouses and Shipwrecks of Isle Royale.* Houghton, Mich.: Isle Royale Natural History Association, 1985.

Kohl, Johann Georg. *Kitchi-Gami: Life Among the Lake Superior Ojibway.* London: Chapman and Hall, 1860. Reprinted in 1985 by the Minnesota Historical Society Press.

Littlejohn, Bruce, and Drew, Wayland. *Superior: The Haunted Shore.* Toronto: Macmillan of Canada, 1983.

Nute, Grace Lee. *Lake Superior.* New York: Bobbs-Merrill, 1944.

―――. *The Voyageur.* New York: D. Appleton, 1931. Reprinted in 1979 by the Minnesota Historical Society Press.

Ratigan, William. *Great Shipwrecks and Survivals.* New York: Galahad Books, 1960.

Roosevelt, Robert Barnwell. *Superior Fishing.* New York: G. W. Carleton, 1865. Reprinted 1985 by the Minnesota Historical Society Press.

Ross, Hamilton Nelson. *La Pointe: Village Outpost.* Private Printing, 1960.

U.S. Department of Transportation. Coast Guard, Marine Casualty Report. *SS Edmund Fitzgerald; Sinking in Lake Superior on 10 November 1975 with Loss of Life.* U.S. Coast Guard Marine Board of Investigation Report and Commandant's Action. Report No. USCG 16732/64216. Washington, D.C., 1977.

U.S. Department of Commerce. National Oceanic and Atmospheric Administration, National Ocean Service. *United States Coast Pilot: Great Lakes.* Washington, D.C.: 1984.

I N D E X

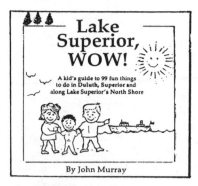

About the author: Marlin Bree, the author of *In the Teeth of the Northeaster*, once lived along Superior's shores and is an inveterate boater. He wrote *Alone Against the Atlantic*, a national best-seller, with sailor Gerry Spiess and served in 1981 as the information officer during Spiess's record crossing of the Pacific in his small boat. In 1992-93, he was a member of the Mike Plant Committee. He is a former editor of the *Star-Tribune's Sunday Magazine* and is a past president of the *Minnesota Press Club*. Bree is a columnist for *Northern Breezes* sailing magazine and is on the book review staff of *Sailing* magazine. He is currently working on a sailing novel.